SMART QUESTIONS

Property Investors
must ask their Solicitor

ROBERT BALANDA

First published in 2013 by Major Street Publishing Pty Ltd
© Robert Balanda 2013
The moral rights of the authors have been asserted.

National Library of Australia Cataloguing-in-Publication data:

Author:	Balanda, Robert author.
Title:	Smart Questions Property Investors Must Ask their Solicitor Robert Balanda.
ISBN:	978-0-9873682-6-3 (pbk.)
Notes:	Includes index.
Subjects:	Real estate investment--Australia.
	Real property--Australia.
	Conveyancing--Australia.
	Lawyers--Australia.
Dewey Number:	332.63247

All rights reserved. Except as permitted under the Australian Copyright Act 1968 (for example, a fair dealing for the purposes of study, research, criticism or review), no part of this book may be reproduced, stored in a retrieval system, communicated or transmitted in any form or by any means without prior written permission. All inquiries should be made to the publisher.

Internal design by Production Works
Cover design by Penny Black Design
Printed in Australia by Griffin Press

10 9 8 7 6 5 4 3 2 1

Disclaimer: The material in this publication is in the nature of general comment only, and neither purports nor intends to be advice. Readers should not act on the basis of any matter in this publication without considering (and if appropriate taking) professional advice with due regard to their own particular circumstances. The author and publisher expressly disclaim all and any liability to any person, whether a purchaser of this publication or not, in respect of anything and the consequences of anything done or omitted to be done by any such person in reliance, whether whole or partial, upon the whole or any part of the contents of this publication.

Purpose: The author and publisher would like to add two important qualifications to the use of this book. Firstly, the book and comments made in it are for educational purposes only and are not provided as specific advice. They should not, therefore, be used without obtaining advice from an experienced property lawyer and taxation accountant and, where appropriate, financial adviser.

Some of the material in this book was first published in the *Australian Property Investor Magazine* (API). Back editions can be purchased by visiting **www.apimagazine.com.au**.

"It is refreshing to read such a down-to-earth book of very helpful hints from a lawyer. It is an easy read and all who are about to buy a property will learn important and potentially money-saving things from the very many hints and simply explained solutions and clauses presented in this unique book. Well done Rob."

John Edwards, Founder of Residex Pty Limited

"This book finally gives to the real estate investing market something that has been missing…an excellent, comprehensive primer on the legal aspects of property transactions for both beginner and experienced investors. Its question and answer format makes it a great and easy read. In particular, I liked the tips on negotiation."

Michael Yardney, Director – Metropole Property Investment Strategists and Best-Selling Author

"I never cease to be amazed that people will spend more than $300,000+ on a property but not $100 on their education. Just one idea can save investors hundreds and thousands of dollars, even more in serious cases, let alone the worry and fear of getting it wrong.

"Smart Questions" has invaluable tips and traps for buyers and sellers. The examples in this book are based on "real life" which makes its purchase a 'no brainer' for property investors. Just get it, use it and you may save yourself a fortune, and even more importantly, keep out of legal trouble."

Geoff Doidge – Reno Kings

About the Author... Robert Balanda

Robert Balanda is a partner of McDonald Balanda & Associates (MBA Lawyers), a four partner medium size legal firm based on the Gold Coast, Queensland. He practises principally in business law, property law, management rights and body corporate law.

Over the last 35 years, Rob Balanda has delivered lectures to groups of investors, real estate agents, business brokers and students on drafting of special conditions for real estate and business contracts and preparation of property documentation such as put and call options, joint venture agreements, co-ownership and asset protection.

Rob Balanda is also the author of the best-selling book, *Clauses Made Simple* and the Made Simple series of property investment products.

Visit www.clausesmadesimple.com for more information.

Contact the Author

If you wish to invite Rob to deliver a presentation to your group, conference or seminar please submit your invitation in writing to him at the address set out below and Rob will respond to your invitation.

MBA Lawyers
PO Box 398
VARSITY LAKES, QLD 4227

To download articles and columns that Rob has published in the *Australian Property Investor Magazine* on property and law visit: **www.clausesmadesimple.com** and click "Articles".

Contents

Preface 1

Part I: Smart Questions to Ask Before You Sign as a Buyer
1. Should I buy in a trust or in my own name? 7
2. Can I use a company to buy property? 10
3. Can I buy in my own name now and change the structure later? 13
4. Who should be trustee of my trust? 14
5. Sharpening your pencil – can one company act as trustee of two trusts? 16
6. Should I get my solicitor's approval before signing a contract? 18
7. Buying property in my child's name – is it a good idea? 19
8. If I am not sure in what name to buy the property, can I add "or nominee" on the contract and decide later? 20
9. How do I select the right solicitor for me? 22

Part II: Smart Questions to Help You Negotiate
10. How do I negotiate in a hot market? 31
11. How do I negotiate with people who aren't sellers? 33
12. What can I do to stop the seller just sitting on my offer? 35
13. What is a sunset clause and when can I use it? 35
14. How do I think outside the square in this market? 38
15. What is a back-up contract and when can I use it? 40
16. A buyer of my property wants to purchase subject to an inspection – what do you think? 41
17. Offers before auction – should I make one? 42
18. The clause you prepared, Rob, was rejected by the seller – what do I do now? 44
19. I am dealing with a town planner from a regional council – do you have any practical tips? 45

v

Part III: Smart Questions about Finance Approval and Vendor Finance
20. My offer is $40k less than the seller is asking. Any tips for bridging the gap? 57
21. Second mortgages – just how good are they? 60
22. Would you use vendor finance to sell a slow-moving property? 61
23. Mortgage protection insurance – what do you think about this way of getting around it? 63
24. Does a finance clause in a contract really allow the buyer to just 'walk away' if they have a change of heart? 65
25. The finance approval from the broker was seven pages long. How do I know if finance is really approved? 67

Part IV: Smart Questions about Units and Body Corporates
26. I am buying a unit in a small block of three units and I am told that there is no body corporate. Is this an issue? 76
27. Do I need to get body corporate approval to keep my cat in this unit that I am buying? 79
28. How do I make sure that all forward bookings of the holiday unit I have just sold are passed on to the buyer? 80
29. How do I deal with a real trouble-maker in my body corporate when I am selling? 81

Part V: Smart Questions About Buying Units Off the Plan
30. Am I protected against building defects when I buy off the plan? 89
31. Under what circumstances can I delay settlement? 91
32. How valuable is a rental guarantee? 92
33. Are there differences for overseas' investors buying off the plan? 95
34. How can I insure against the property losing value before I take possession? 97
35. If I am the second or third buyer off the plan – what are the pitfalls? 101

Part VI: Smart Questions Concerning Deposits

36. Do I need to pay a deposit? **108**
37. How much should the deposit be? **108**
38. Does the deposit have to be in cash? **111**
39. Should I release the deposit before settlement? **112**
40. Should I agree to release of the deposit to allow the seller to buy another property? **114**

Part VII: Smart Questions about Options, Rights of First Refusal and Preliminary Agreements

41. What is the difference between an option and a right of first refusal? **121**
42. Will real estate agents help you find option properties? **123**
43. Why would a seller sign a call option agreement? **124**
44. Where do you find properties over which the sellers might grant you a call option? **124**
45. Preliminary agreements – paperwork worth doing? **125**

Part VIII: Smart Questions about Searches, Investigations and Due Diligence

46. What is a due diligence? **132**
47. Can I apply for building and development approval over a property that I don't yet own? **135**
48. Pest and building inspections – what are the traps with the standard clauses in contracts used by agents? **137**
49. Thermal imaging – what will it pick up that my builder might miss? **139**
50. Zoning – how important is it? **140**
51. When do I need to make my contract subject to an environmental check? **141**
52. When is fire safety an issue? **143**
53. How important is it to do a survey on a property? **144**
54. How do I check who really owns the plant and equipment on this farm I am buying? **145**
55. Should I be concerned about floods and other natural disasters? **146**

Part IX: Smart Questions About Leases and Tenancies

56. I am buying a property with a tenant – what are the traps? **153**
57. Should I allow the seller to remain in possession after settlement? **154**
58. Is it true that the lease of a commercial property is everything? **155**
59. Is it hard to sack your letting agent? **157**

Part X: More Smart Questions

60. How can I get access to a property before the settlement date? **164**
61. What are my rights as a buyer of a property to get an early settlement? **164**
62. What risk do I carry as a buyer of a property after the contract is signed? **165**
63. I have been asked to be a token director of my friend's company – what do you think? **166**
64. Tired of the treadmill of buy, renovate, sell – is it really all worth it? **168**
65. This development site has gone up so much. Should I just sell it and forget developing it? **169**
66. Depreciation and negative gearing – are the benefits really just a myth? **171**
67. How Does GST affect a valuation? **172**
68. This developer has DA approval, but now wants to sell without developing. How can I benefit if I now buy off the developer? **173**
69. Personal guarantees – what do I need to check? **175**
70. Trading properties – what are the pitfalls for the unwary? **176**
71. What items are included in the sale? **178**
72. Should I consider a tempting new financial product? **179**
73. Powers of Attorney – do I need one? **181**
74. Breakdown of appliances before settlement – who is responsible? **181**
75. What state should the property be in on settlement? **182**

Preface

The aim of this book is to help you become the best generalist that you can be.

Some investors devour every bit of information about property investment they can in the same way people fall in love with their football team or their kid's school. Others take the minimalist approach about their general education, discarding anything that they don't need to know on the basis that they'll engage experts to do it for them when it's necessary.

I'm a strong believer in becoming the best generalist that you can be, as this philosophy will stand you in better stead. I, therefore, encourage readers to become engaged investors. Learn about trades, options and such things as vendor finance, even if you don't have the intention of using any of these strategies or concepts. Exploring these concepts and strategies gives greater power to you as an investor because it creates an attitude towards education that will serve you better.

The last time I got on my soapbox about this issue, someone with the contrarian view challenged me with: "Why bark when you've got a dog?" This was the blunt response from a couple of investors to me, one of whom was a specialist mortgage broker and the other an accountant. They said they felt they were "smarter than the average bear" because they had specialist knowledge in a related field to property investment, so my strategy didn't apply to them. They couldn't be more wrong. In fact, I believe the reverse is true.

As a specialist, you have a high degree of knowledge and this has a tendency to blinker and even blind you to an opportunity. Often, therefore, opportunities will go flying by and be missed by you as a specialist because you're looking at the issue through the filters of your specialist knowledge. Contrast that with the approach of a generalist whose general awareness about property has been raised to allow them to spot opportunities that then become so obvious to them.

In essence, then, becoming a generalist will serve you better and will build a confidence that will embolden and enrich you. So when you read this book, read every chapter. If at first you are tempted to skip a smart question, ask yourself this smart question: "Will this information add to my general knowledge as an investor?" If so, read on.

A $10,000 mistake in property investment may seem a small mistake. But there's a way to avoid losing money in your property investing transactions and that is to educate yourself first. Put the time and the effort into preparing yourself for property investing and this will go a long way to minimising mistakes. It will also make the whole experience a lot more enjoyable.

In this book, I have put together real-life questions that every property investor should ask their solicitor. Specialist property solicitors working in this area charge anything from $300 to $400 per hour. This book is a fraction of the cost. Reading it is a smart way of educating yourself about property investment before taking the plunge – much better to do that than just parachute into unfamiliar territory.

Experienced property investors, too, will learn a lot from reading this book as it will help them realise what they didn't know.

So absorb the lessons from SMART QUESTIONS like your mother's milk. All of them have been learnt by someone else first – the hard way. Good luck with your property investment.

Although I practise law in Queensland, this book is relevant Australia-wide. The advice contained in it is general and not specific to your circumstances so, although it will help you a great deal with legal matters, you may need to consult a lawyer in your own state on your own particular circumstances.

ROB BALANDA
March 2013

Part I
SMART QUESTIONS TO ASK BEFORE YOU SIGN AS A BUYER

Blessed are they who go around in circles. For they shall be known as big wheels.

ANONYMOUS

Smart Questions to Ask Before You Sign as a Buyer

Many investors sacrifice quality for speed and blunder into a new territory like property investment without taking proper advice. There are some elementary issues that you should always consider before you enter into a contract to purchase real estate. First and foremost is what entity to use to buy the property.

The fundamental choices are whether to buy the property in your own name personally, in the name of a company or in the name of a person or company acting as trustee for some type of trust.

The reason why you need to get this fundamental issue right from the start is that to un-do it, and remedy a mistake made in selecting the wrong entity after signing a contract, can be extremely expensive. It could be a mistake for which you pay dearly. Transfer of a property into the correct entity, following a misstep by you in acquiring it in the wrong name initially, will generate serious additional legal fees. These will pale, though, into nothing when compared to additional stamp duty and possible GST and capital gains tax obligations. The problem just compounds, as acquiring the property in the wrong name can also lead to the annual loss of taxation benefits, e.g. the imposition of higher rates of tax which you shouldn't have paid if you had chosen the proper structure. There may be a lost opportunity to use negative gearing losses and last but not least, you may be left without any asset protection and exposed personally to a claim by some greedy litigant looking to "have a go".

Therefore, in this first part of the book, I set out the initial round of smart questions that you should ask your solicitor which revolve around the entity to be utilised to purchase the property. Of course, as with all the 75 questions in the book, I answer them too!

Remember always that investing in property without first educating yourself is a recipe for a storm. Education is your bridge and safe crossing into the real world of property. So put the time and money into educating yourself now. Remember, too, that no lender or divorce court can ever take that education away from you.

> *"George Mumble, the home county's most henpecked husband, died today. By the terms of his will, his ashes will be scattered all over his wife's new living room carpet."*
> THE TWO RONNIES

1 SHOULD I BUY IN A TRUST OR IN MY OWN NAME?

An investor client, let's call him Paul, recently gave me the go-ahead to acquire a company for him. This company would act as trustee for a family trust which I was to create in due course, once he'd taken further advice from his accountant about the matter. The next time I heard from Paul was after he'd been to a property investment seminar where he and the other attendees were told they'd been duped into believing the best way to buy property was in the name of a company acting as trustee for a trust. The advice from the presenter at the seminar was that it was best to keep things simple and just buy property in your own names, but protect yourself by getting the best insurance possible.

He'd been told that personal ownership of assets was important and something which he, as an Australian, should be proud of. The presenter said people who promoted companies and trusts were doing so to promote their professional services and products. This led Paul to ask me which path he should follow. I told him that in my opinion the company/trust structure still looks like ownership, smells like ownership and feels like ownership but doesn't have that sting in the tail of having personal liability. A company/trust structure means you can deal with the asset as if you own it, but without any personal liability or exposing youself to greedy litigants and predators. In addition, buying in your own name limits your flexibility in dealing with the income from an investment property and any capital gain made on its sale.

A company/trust structure allows you to distribute this income and gain to the person with the greatest tax benefits at the time.

2 CAN I USE A COMPANY TO BUY PROPERTY?

I received a phone call from an established client who wanted to buy an investment unit in a new company (and not as a trustee for a trust). A friend of his had just bought a company "off the shelf" but could no longer use it and was now looking to "offload it". The company was for sale for next to nothing and he believed it would be a great idea to buy a property in a company name for asset protection and taxation purposes. Wrong!

I educated him about the fact that a company can often be the worst vehicle to acquire real estate for a number of reasons. Firstly, any income received from rental, or any capital gain made on the sale of the property, would be taxed at the fixed rate of 30 cents in every dollar (the current company tax rate). Secondly, the 50 per cent concession on capital gains tax (if you sell a property at a profit after holding it for more than a year) doesn't apply to companies – only individuals and trusts. After exploring his financial position I advised him that the best vehicle to use to purchase the property would be a company acting as trustee for a trust.

Ever keen to save a dollar, he then suggested that he buy the property in the name of the company acting as trustee for his family trust which operated his manufacturing business. Once again, wrong! Running a business in Australia carries with it inherent risks that someone may sue you one day. Placing more assets into a company/trust structure that operates a business is just not a smart move.

From an asset protection perspective, it increases the amount of any likely claim by a greedy litigant. My advice to him was to spend another $2,000 and acquire a brand new company and trust and buy the property in that company acting in its trustee capacity, thus quarantining his real estate asset from his business operations and giving him much greater asset protection.

So, asset-protect yourself

Those of us who've had a few runs around the block will remember the case that ran through the Australian courts some years ago. A husband and wife had structured themselves years earlier with their property investments so that all assets were in the wife's name. The reason was that the husband had a very high-risk job. Then the wife was out on the golf course playing golf one afternoon when one of her misdirected golf balls hit a man in the head causing him serious injuries. As a result the injured man sued her for a lot of money, and he was successful.

This case changed the whole landscape about asset protection and got people for the first time to start using entities, such as companies and trusts, when they'd never done so before, solely for the purpose of asset protection.

The case is a timely reminder to us that it's therefore not just a matter of trusting your spouse when it comes to asset protection. Accidents do happen.

You need, therefore, to establish company/trust structures

to buy your investment properties and hold as little as possible in any personal name. The basic strategy is based on there being no legal liability back to you from the entities that own the assets.

It's a good idea to have a careful look at who really is at risk here. I believe that anyone who owns assets personally in Australia is at risk. So why then do we continue to hold assets in personal names? It's a middle class attitude that has something to do with pride of ownership. But what it really does is expose us to greedy predators looking to have a go. By the same token, don't despair if you already own a number of properties in personal names. Asset protection is a process.

Timing is important, though, and the sooner you asset-protect yourself the better. However, changing structures and entities in which you hold properties is costly and can often trigger payment of GST and capital gains tax and lose you the benefit of land tax exemptions. You might therefore retain properties you own in personal names now and with new purchases implement asset-protection strategies by buying them in the name of a company acting as trustee for a trust.

Over time you might be able to undo the exposure you have with holding properties in personal names, so don't despair about it too much. Remember, too, that ownership in a company or trust structure still looks like ownership, smells like ownership and feels like ownership but it doesn't have that sting in the tail of personal liability when the property is owned in your name. You don't own the asset personally but instead you control it through share holdings and directorships of the company that manages the trust.

3 CAN I BUY IN MY OWN NAME NOW AND CHANGE THE STRUCTURE LATER?

Investors frequently say to me "Rob, you worry too much. Let's buy this property now in my name personally and if ever anyone sues me I can at that time transfer the property to some other entity e.g. a company/trust structure".

What are the risks of going down this path? One unfortunate Australian taxpayer recently found out and ended up spending two years in prison contemplating the risks of this approach. The taxpayer was a director of his own company which had received a large taxation bill. The company's assets were sold to pay the bill but the proceeds were not enough to discharge the liability to the Australian Tax Office (ATO). As a director of the company he knew he had a personal liability to the ATO but he transferred his interest in a property in his own name to another party to avoid the trustee in bankruptcy getting at this asset (the ATO bankrupted him over the tax liability).

The strategy appeared to be "Let's transfer the property and see if the trustee in bankruptcy goes to the trouble and expense of attempting to recover the proceeds of the sale".

What this man and his adviser probably didn't realise was that such a transfer constitutes a criminal offence under the *Bankruptcy Act*. That Act provides that when a person goes bankrupt, and within 12 months before that date disposes of any property with intent to defraud the creditor (e.g. the ATO), they are guilty of an offence which carries a prison sentence of up to three years. The taxpayer was convicted of this offence and was sentenced to two years jail.

4 WHO SHOULD BE TRUSTEE OF MY TRUST?

"Should I personally be a trustee of my trust?"

This is a perfectly sensible question. After all, a company costs around $700 to acquire and involves paying annual charges to ASIC (Australian Securities and Investments Commission) and usually additional accountancy fees.

I don't recommend this approach for two reasons. The first reason is that trustees run the trust and are entitled to an indemnity for their actions from the trust, backed up by whatever assets the trust owns. But if the trustees are individuals then they expose themselves personally if there's a shortfall in the trust assets to meet any liability. Contrast this with operating as a director of a trustee company where there's no personal liability as the director and no exposure of your own assets unless you, as a director, allow the company to trade insolvent.

The second reason isn't as obvious. When I discuss this matter with lawyers who act for potential litigants, they advise me that where a person acts as trustee for a trust it sends a clear message to them that they may be vulnerable because they're so cost-sensitive, (i.e. they didn't want to spend the $700 to get a company trustee). They will seriously then discuss with their client the possibility of bringing an action against that person, just to put pressure on them so that they'll make an offer of money to make the problem go away. The lawyers' experiences are that these people will be so worried about the cost of defending the action that they'll be likely to make an offer to pay some money just to get you to go away.

In essence, then, a company/trust structure still looks like ownership, smells like ownership and feels like ownership, but doesn't have that sting in the tail of having personal liability. A company/trust structure means you can deal with the assets as if you own them, but without any personal liability or exposure.

Understand the structure

I took a phone call from a new client who'd been to a high-powered property investment seminar and heard a wonderful presentation on asset protection by an accountant who specialised in establishing companies and trusts. He jumped in after the seminar and immediately purchased a company and trust.

His next call to me was to make an appointment and at that appointment he asked, "Could you please explain what I've just bought and how it works? Most importantly, could you please tell me what name I should put on the contract as the buyer of this property that I wish to acquire, now that I have this company/ trust structure? Should I show the buyer as just the company, or the company as trustee and do I need to specifically mention the name of the trust?"

The client could be forgiven for such naivety but I was appalled that a professional could allow a client to acquire such a structure without ensuring that he or she had a sound understanding of how it operates.

If you find yourself in this situation as an investor, insist that the adviser/accountant/lawyer spend time with you so that when you leave their office you understand what you've just acquired. Otherwise there'll be GST consequences, CGT consequences and other undesirable outcomes such as drawing cheques from the wrong accounts. These could be very difficult or even impossible to undo at a later stage.

And where are you as an investor when you find yourself in this position? Lost is the answer.

It's time to go back to basics – understand the structure.

5 SHARPENING YOUR PENCIL – CAN ONE COMPANY ACT AS TRUSTEE OF TWO TRUSTS?

In a slowing market, investors tend to become more cost-conscious, as illustrated by a recent query from a new client, let's call her Mary. Mary had already acquired three properties in the name of a company acting as trustee for her family trust (for asset protection purposes). Now, she consulted me about acquiring the next three properties in the name of another trust.

Mary's query was: "Should I set up another company to act as trustee for the second trust or can I use the first company to act as trustee for the second trust as well? I'm worried firstly about the additional costs of setting up this second company but also the ongoing additional annual fees for my accountant and annual return fees to ASIC. If we make it clear which trust the company is acting for, does that not allow me to use the one company as trustee for two different trusts and still retain the full benefit of asset protection?"

In short the answer is, "No, not completely." My advice to Mary was not to be penny-pinching and to spend the extra money to buy the second company (and pay the ongoing annual fees) for the following reasons.

The asset-protection strategy here is to buy three properties, say in the name of one company as trustee for a trust. The next three properties should be acquired in the name of another company acting as trustee for a second trust. The strategy is about risk minimisation and in particular about spreading the risk. The theory is that if somebody is looking at having a go at you, they would firstly sue the company (which has two $1 shares as its only assets). If they get behind that company then they can have a go at the trust, which will own a maximum of three properties. The creditor can't touch any of the assets owned by the other company and trust.

If, however, you use one company as trustee for multiple trusts you undermine that strategy. You create the impression that the company as trustee has more than three properties, i.e. it has six properties now which are exposed to a potential claim. You also send a clear signal to someone looking at having a go that you are cost-conscious and therefore are vulnerable to a claim by someone hoping to get some "go-away money" from you to drop their claim. That is, in return for say $20,000 or $30,000 they won't continue what they know to be a baseless claim.

It is silly to put yourself in that position for the sake of one initial fee of say $700 and annual fees only running into hundreds of dollars a year.

6 SHOULD I GET MY SOLICITOR'S APPROVAL BEFORE SIGNING A CONTRACT?

If you see a property on a Saturday afternoon and you want to make an offer to buy it, but baulk at signing a contract before your solicitor has checked it on Monday, why not sign the contract with a special condition which makes it subject to your solicitor's approval by 5pm on Monday. Most sellers will sign on this basis and at least then the property will be taken off the market so that it cannot be purchased by someone else on the Sunday or on Monday before you get to see your solicitor.

In practice, nine times out of ten the solicitor will sign off on the contract before 5pm on Monday. A cynic would reject the clause outright, however I have used it many times and almost invariably the contract was approved by the solicitor concerned.

An appropriate clause would be the following:

> "This Contract is subject to the Buyer's solicitor approving of the terms of the Contract of Sale by 5.00pm on the (complete) day of (complete) 20(complete), failing which

this Contract will be at an end, the Deposit refunded to the Buyer and neither party will have any claim against the other apart from any rights either of the parties will have against the other as a result of any breach of this Contract.

The Buyer must advise the Seller in writing within one (1) working day of the (complete) day of (complete) 20__ (complete) whether this clause has been satisfied or the benefit of it is waived."

7 BUYING PROPERTY IN MY CHILD'S NAME – IS IT A GOOD IDEA?

A call came through from my receptionist and I spoke to an enthusiastic but misguided Mum and Dad wanting to buy a property in their daughter's name. "Better to give with a warm hand than a cold hand," they said (meaning, give it to the child now rather than leave it to them in their will). "It's not as simple as that," I said. "Let me take you through all of the dimensions of buying real estate in the name of a child."

The starting point *is* that it is legal to do it. The Titles Office will register a transfer of a property into a child's name and the Title Deed will show the owner as, for example, "Isabella Seymour, a minor born on March 1, 2006". The property, however, can't be sold, mortgaged or dealt with in any way until your child reaches the age of 18 (unless you get approval from the Supreme Court to do so – which would be extremely unlikely and very expensive to try). When Isabella turns 18, if you produce a birth certificate to the Titles Office it will register a Departmental Dealing over the property and remove the words "a minor born on March 1, 2006" – and presto, your "Bella Principessa" (means beautiful princess for all you people who only read magazines) is the proud owner of an unencumbered piece of real estate, without incurring any stamp duty and after payment of a modest Titles Office fee only.

What damage can that girl do now?

Whoa! Party time!

Now, Dad was an accountant and after I gave him the explanation outlined above, he said to me, "OK, let's buy the property in my name as trustee for the child". The trust arrangement, he said, could be set out in writing and state that the property would vest in her at the age of 21 (not 18) when, as readers know, she's more likely to spend her newfound wealth on a Porsche and designer clothes rather than party it away on alcohol. "Up until 21," Dad said, "I can still deal with the property without Supreme Court approval as the property will still be registered in my name (as trustee)". "Ah", I said to Dad, "but when she turns 21 you'll have to pay the full rate of stamp duty (based on the property market value when the girl turns 21) to transfer the property into her name. And you can take your own advice as an accountant about what capital gains tax is payable on the transfer of property 20 years later at a much increased value."

Let's not overlook the tax consequences of buying a property in the name of a minor. The first $1,300 of the rental income will be tax-free but after that it's taxed at the penalty rate (minimum of 45 cents in the dollar at time of writing). So, at the end of the day, buying a property in a child's name doesn't have much going for it.

8 IF I AM NOT SURE IN WHAT NAME TO BUY THE PROPERTY, CAN I ADD "OR NOMINEE" ON THE CONTRACT AND DECIDE LATER?

An investor sought my advice about a hot property he'd found that was going to auction the following day. Time was of the essence and the investor wanted to buy the property before the auction. He was just about to submit an offer to purchase the property when he had reservations about what name to buy it in. He called his accountant but she was on holidays. His next call was to me. "Could I draft a clause to be included in the contract that would allow me the right to elect to buy the property in another name after consulting my accountant on her return from holidays?" "Certainly", I said, "however, you should be aware that in Queensland if you do elect to buy the property in another name, up to an additional 100 per cent stamp duty will be payable on the sale on the basis that the Office of State Revenue maintains that exercising the nominee and buying in another name is deemed to be another sale of the property."

The moral of the story is that he should have taken professional advice well before that day about what entity he should use to buy the property. The clause I suggested he add to the contract to give him the right to nominate another party (and not be beholden to the seller to do so) is set out below. It should be understood, though, that this clause would give you the right to nominate another party to buy, if you did so in Queensland, double stamp duty would be payable.

"A. The buyer may appoint a nominee to purchase the property (nominee may include the buyer) by giving to the seller or the seller's solicitor notice in writing of such nomination.

B. If the buyer appoints a nominee, the nominee will be entitled to exercise all of the rights of the buyer under this contract as if it was the buyer except for the right to appoint a further nominee in terms of this clause.

C. If the buyer appoints a nominee, the buyer guarantees the performance of the nominee's obligations under this contract including the payment of all monies payable under this contract, and the buyer indemnifies the seller from any liability, costs, loss or damage incurred by the seller arising out of any failure by the nominee to perform its obligations under this contract or breach of its obligations."

9 HOW DO I SELECT THE RIGHT SOLICITOR FOR ME?

One way to avoid painful and costly mistakes as an investor is to engage a competent solicitor to advise you at the start of the contract negotiation process. I'm often asked at presentations that I deliver around the country: "How do I go about finding a solicitor in my area who's right for my needs?" It's essential when selecting a solicitor that you engage someone who will act always in your best interests, without the fear of upsetting or offending someone else in the transaction, particularly the real estate agent.

I recommend that you tackle the issue in this way.

Ask around your circle of friends and fellow investors for

the name of a solicitor that they have used personally for their real estate investments. Interview the solicitor personally, but don't tell them that you will be interviewing them. Any solicitor worth their salt will have plenty of work to do and if you tell them you want to interview them to decide whether you are going to select them as your solicitor they won't be interested. To put it simply and from their perspective, why should they spend valuable fee-earning time talking to you when they already have fee-paying files sitting on their desk that they could work on? I suggest you tell the solicitor that they have been recommended to you by someone (and give that person's name) and that you would like to make an appointment to talk to them about your property investments.

First question you should ask the solicitor is: "Do you invest in real estate yourself?" If the answer is no, you are dealing with the wrong professional. How can they be expected to understand and appreciate issues with your real estate investments if they have no such investments themselves. Seek out another solicitor.

If the answer to the first question is yes, ask them whether they do the work personally. If they don't do the work personally, then ask to speak to the person who does and start back at question one.

Ask the solicitor whether they handle the work on a daily basis. The last thing you want to do is to be dealing with a middle-aged professional who over the last 20 years has been a family law specialist, but has lost his last five major cases in the family law arena. The word has spread amongst the people who refer him business and his source of work has dried up. He's looking to re-train himself in real estate work. You don't want him learning on the job while handling your files.

Ask the solicitor whether they accept referrals from the agent that you are dealing with. If they receive 20 or 30 referrals from that agent every year, should some issue arise where they will have to stand up for you without fear or favour, will they do so? Or, are they the agent's friend and they'll look for some simple, expeditious solution that allows the matter to proceed so the agent collects their commission?

The cynics amongst you might be thinking, "Just a minute, haven't solicitors got ethical standards to adhere to and shouldn't they always be acting in my best interests if I'm paying the bill?" Unfortunately, this is a somewhat naïve view. The reality is that they are in business too and survive in business like all of us by building and maintaining relationships and associations. It is possible that preserving that relationship may be more important to them than standing up for your rights.

Should I use the same solicitor as the seller on my purchase?

There's synchronicity in the property world. I stepped down from a stage after a presentation to a group of investors recently and was startled by the continuing need that investors have to remind themselves of the basics about property investment.

A young couple were first to approach me and their position illustrates my comments perfectly. They'd just reached agreement a day or two earlier on the purchase of a property and their first mistake was that they'd been persuaded by the real estate agent to engage the services of a solicitor to handle their purchase of the property who was in the same firm as the solicitors for the seller. They were assured that the two solicitors were in separate offices (cynically described by lawyers as 'Chinese walls') and they would be represented independently by that solicitor without any interference, fear or favour to the seller or the selling agent.

They were advised, too, that they would acquire this property subject to a lease which the agent said could be terminated at any time. They hadn't been provided with a copy of the lease to verify this representation and I was alarmed when they told me that the tenant was very good friends with the seller. Someone fearing the worst might be deeply suspicious in these circumstances about what sweetheart deal had been done between the seller and the tenant (whom you'll inherit because leases 'run with the land').

Of course, no mention was made by the agent about adding a clause to the contract to make it subject to the buyer and their solicitor being satisfied about the terms of this lease, which was particularly important here as the investors had told the agent they wanted to move into the property a month after settlement and were assured there would be no problems in doing so.

To compound things further, the contract was to be subject to a pest and building inspection and the agent had recommended a pest and building inspector to the buyer who was well known to the agent because of the agent's personal relationship. The inspector had also committed to undertaking the job at a very keen price.

"It sounds like one of those tick-box inspection reports to me," I said, "where the most basic of investigations only would be carried out".

The inspector wouldn't want to ruffle any feathers of the referring agent whom he'd be relying on for another 20 or 30 referrals that year, now would he?

So if a problem came up, would the builder look for a quick fix or soft solution, or stand up for you without fear or favour?

At the end of the day, who was looking after the interests of these investors?

This is why self-education is so important.

> *"I don't like all this fresh air. I'm from Los Angeles. I don't trust an air I can't see."*
> BOB HOPE (1903-2003),
> AMERICAN COMEDIAN AND ACTOR

Part II
SMART QUESTIONS TO HELP YOU NEGOTIATE

First you forget names, then you forget faces. Next you forget to pull your zipper up and, finally, you forget to pull it down.

GEORGE BURNS, AMERICAN COMEDIAN

Smart Questions to Help You Negotiate

My catchcry is "Education, Education, Education". The expectation in the property world is that you will do well at property investment but this expectation isn't matched by the reality because of the lack of education. Nowhere is this more apparent than in the area of negotiation. All too often I see investors led by the nose by a more skilful negotiator (the seller's real estate agent) to agree to the terms of a deal which a more street-smart and property-savvy investor would have rejected. In my opinion, therefore, the single most important skill for an investor is the skill of a good negotiator.

It is no surprise that Robert Kiyosaki, the author of *Rich Dad, Poor Dad* says that unless you know how to negotiate you will never get rich. So put the effort into becoming a better negotiator and it will pay off handsomely for you.

Before I answer the smart questions to help you negotiate, here are a few general negotiating tips.

1. Always be careful not to get personal with your negotiating style. John Potter, master negotiator and author of the book *A Property Investor's Guide to Negotiating* believes that having a philosophy of, "Give no offence, and take none" will serve you well in property investment. John Potter also says: "So, as

a buyer, don't describe the property as a 'dog box' or 'nothing more than a demolition job'. None of these comments are helpful or likely to secure you a reduction in the price. You're better served if you tell the seller of the property that it's a good property and has potential but it's obviously in need of work to bring it up to its best state, which will cost say around $30,000, and therefore your offer to buy is made on that basis.

2. Remember to never be too urgent to do a deal. Show that you're ready to negotiate a contract, but don't seem too desperate to do so.
3. Promote yourself (as a buyer) as someone who's an empathetic listener. Let sellers talk as much as they want and listen as much as you can.
4. Finally, never say "it's not personal". The other party will always respond with, "Yes it is!"

> *"Prince Charles is planning to record his own version of Frank Sinatra's hit, 'My Way'. He is going to call it 'One Did it One's Way'."*
> NEIL SHAND, ENGLISH COMEDIAN

10 HOW DO I NEGOTIATE IN A HOT MARKET?

My first call early one Monday morning was from a disgruntled and frustrated investor. He had made five offers to buy properties over the weekend (all in "hot spots") only to be told by the agent that the property had either sold as soon as it had listed or they already had multiple offers at the listed price. "I would love to jump on the property train", he said, "If only it would slow down long enough for me to get a foothold." I agreed with his sentiment that in some markets it is just often a matter of, "He who throws the most money at the seller gets the property". He then asked did I have any suggestions how he might improve his negotiating to buy property in this "hot" market.

Although his question was not a legal question for a solicitor, I was able to help him.

I told him that I recently found myself in the same situation when negotiating to buy a property for two companies. The property was listed for sale at $350,000 and I made an offer for the asking price, subject to finance, pest and building inspections and due diligence (to check the agent's representation that the property would take three units). The settlement date for my offer was 90 days from the date of the contract. Within two days of making the offer the agent advised me that he had six other offers for the property, all at the asking price and all subject to various special conditions and with settlement between 60 and 90 days. He was going to submit all of the offers to the seller and asked me did I want to alter my contract in any way.

I asked him what I needed to do to get the edge and he would not give me the slightest hint. I asked him to hold off seeing the seller for a couple of hours and advised him that I would come back to him with an amended offer.

My next call was to a bank manager to confirm that he would finance the purchase and therefore I did not need the protection of a finance clause. The following telephone call was to a town planner who confirmed that I could construct three units on the site, and perhaps even up to five units. I therefore did not need the protection of a due diligence clause. Neither did I need the protection of a pest and building inspection clause as the dwelling on the property would ultimately be demolished.

I then submitted a revised offer to the agent for a purchase price of $375,000, with a 10 per cent deposit, with no special conditions (that is, a "cash" contract), with settlement to be within 30 days from the date of the contract. I also attached a waiver of the cooling off period.

The offer was accepted by the seller.

Before settlement I thought that I had better "back-test" my strategy and I asked the agent what came of the other five or six offers, and why my offer was accepted. The agent's advice confirmed my previous experiences with real estate agents. In a scenario such as this their usual strategy (when having multiple competing buyers) is to edge each of them up on their price in increments, in this case of say, $5,000 at a time until there was ultimately only one buyer standing who would buy the property at the maximum price that the market would pay (usually giving away most of the future profits in so doing). My strategy in making the amended offer was to secure the property at a price that still allowed me to make a profit but not get me involved in a "Dutch Auction" (see Question 12), where the agent uses your offer to force another potential buyer to increase their offer, and then use that increased offer to force you and others to further increase the sale price of the property.

The agent advised me that he believed he could get two or three of the potential buyers to increase their offer by $5,000 to $10,000 and one of the potential buyers would probably have gone up another $15,000 (to $365,000). However, when I came in with my offer of $375,000 he was confident that none of the other buyers would match it. He therefore advised the seller not to play around with my excellent offer, to accept it and reject all of the others. In essence then my offer blew the other buyers away without giving all of my profit away. Before the settlement of the purchase I received an offer to buy the property for $395,000, thus justifying my strategy and the ultimate purchase price of $375,000.

11 HOW DO I NEGOTIATE WITH PEOPLE WHO AREN'T SELLERS?

A local solicitor (who wasn't a property lawyer) approached me for some guidance about how to deal with a difficult situation. He was attempting to buy a property in a country town with a seller who didn't have the property listed for sale but was prepared to entertain an offer. He'd submitted an offer of $220,000 and the owner told the real estate agent this was not enough.

The agent then suggested the owner make a counter-offer and sign the contract for a higher price that would be acceptable to him. "No way", the seller said, "he's come to me with this offer and it's up to him to increase the offer. Just tell your buyer client that", said the owner. "Come back with a higher offer and I'll consider that."

What should the prospective buyer do now? Classic negotiating theory will tell you that he shouldn't make another offer following a previous offer unless the other party has made some concession or counter-offer.

My friend was prepared to make a small increase to his offer but didn't want to fall into the ever-increasing spiral downwards of making offer after offer without acceptance or counter-offer by the seller, only to find that he eventually paid far too much for the property and gave away most of his profit.

My advice to him was that when he made his second offer, presuming the seller rejected it without making a counter-offer, he should tell the agent to go back with his second offer and do his job. He should get the seller to make a counter-offer, or otherwise withdraw his offer. To do anything else would see the seller eventually take advantage of him. The only alternative was (if the agent was again unsuccessful in getting the seller to countersign the contract) to withdraw from the process because while he was a "buyer", the owner wasn't yet a "seller". The owner hadn't really decided to sell and was just playing around with him. You're wasting your time dealing with someone who isn't a "seller".

12 WHAT CAN I DO TO STOP THE SELLER JUST SITTING ON MY OFFER?

Ever found yourself in a Dutch auction? As we explained in Question 10, this is a situation where you, as a buyer, believe the seller may be using your offer to force another potential buyer to increase their offer and then, in turn, be using their increased offer to put pressure on you to increase your offer. Why not add a special clause to the contract restricting their ability to do so?

This clause could also be used where you believe your offer may "linger" because the seller simply sits on it for days or where there are multiple offers coming in on a property that you are chasing. How do you get to the head of the queue? The clause that will achieve the result you need is one that will force the seller to accept the offer in writing by a certain time or else the offer is withdrawn. Here is such a clause:

> "The offer to purchase this property contained in this contract will lapse unless written notice of acceptance of it is received by the buyer or the buyer's solicitor by no later than 5pm on the (insert date)."

13 WHAT IS A SUNSET CLAUSE AND WHEN CAN I USE IT?

In an upward-trending real estate market, it's often a case of, "He who throws the most money at a property gets it".

However, in a softening market, investors need to be more creative and street-smart to bring a deal together. That's the time then to revisit an old chestnut, the sunset clause.

Traditionally a sunset clause is used in a down-trending or flat market to achieve a sale. The clause deals with an impasse where a seller is reluctant to accept a conditional offer to purchase their property because of the belief that a higher offer may be forthcoming from someone else shortly.

In these cases, the buyers may be unwilling to offer more, and in any event might also need to protect themselves by entering into a conditional contract, for example by making their offer to purchase subject to procuring a contract of sale on their own property. The solution is to insert a sunset clause which provides that if the seller receives another written offer on better terms from another buyer (and they must prove this by providing a copy of the contracts and receipt for the deposit) then the seller can give the buyer, say, four working days' notice that they want them to waive the benefit of the "subject to" clause and go unconditional, or the contract is at an end.

Investors generally understand that this solution has a downside for the seller, which is that if they secure a cash contract for a better price they can't then force the buyers to match the second offer. All they can do is force the sellers to go unconditional. What investors don't generally understand, however, is that this clause also has a downside for a buyer. Once this downside is appreciated then the parties will truly understand that the clause is genuine and a fair compromise between the interests of both the buyer and the seller, and therefore they should both be encouraged to consider it as a way of moving forward in the real estate market.

The way this clause is weighted against the buyer is that the existence of the contract in the marketplace gives greater confidence to other potential buyers and in reality pushes other buyers to offer more, thus placing pressure on the buyer to achieve a sale of their own property sooner rather than later (and probably for a lesser price rather than a greater price).

Here is a sample sunset clause:

"(a) Should the seller receive another written offer to purchase their property in the form of a binding and enforceable Contract of Sale signed by the proposed buyer; and

(b) The Contract of Sale is not subject to finance or settlement of the sale of another property; and

(c) The proposed buyer has paid a deposit of ten per cent (10%) of the purchase price being a purchase price not less than $(insert amount), then the seller will notify the buyer or the buyer's solicitors in writing of that offer.

The Seller will also provide to the buyer or the buyer's solicitors a copy of the signed Contract of Sale together with a copy of the trust account receipt from the agent or Deposit Holder on that sale for the deposit.

The buyer will have seven (7) days from receipt by them or their solicitors of the copy of Contract of Sale and copy of receipt for the deposit to advise the seller in writing that he waives the benefit of condition(s) (insert number of any special conditions) of this Contract failing which this Contract will be at an end, the deposit will be refunded to the buyer and neither party will have any claim against the other apart from any rights either of the parties may have against the other as a result of any breach of this Contract."

14. HOW DO I THINK OUTSIDE THE SQUARE IN THIS MARKET?

In a softening market, buyers expect that bargains and opportunities abound – but do they really? Sometimes this isn't the reality, as sellers struggle to accept the correction in the market and the fact that if they want to sell their property they'll have to drop their price. Therefore, buyers still have to be creative in presenting their offers to purchase and in particular in drawing special clauses for contracts for sale.

Thinking more creatively may just give you the edge and secure the property for you. As a solicitor you're never surprised about the variety of instructions you receive from investors and the different style of clauses clients use to record the terms of the agreement they've reached with the other party. Nonetheless, the following clause does make for interesting reading:

> "1. Subject to Valuation
>
> The Seller acknowledges that the Buyer wishes to undertake a valuation of the property by a Valuer of his/her choice but who must be a Valuer whose firm is on the panel of Valuers engaged by the Buyer's lender. This contract is subject to the Buyer being satisfied with the valuation undertaken by the Valuer selected by him/her within 14 days from the date of this contract, failing which the Buyer may terminate this Contract. In that event this matter will be at an end, the deposit refunded to the Buyer and no party will have a claim against the other in relation to this Contract, except a claim based on a breach by one of the parties of their obligations under this Contract prior to the date of termination.

2. Purchase Price

The purchase price of the property will be the value of the property determined by the Buyer's Valuer pursuant to special condition 1 above, *less an amount equal to 10 per cent* of the amount of that valuation.

3. Subject to Approval of Valuation

This Contract is also subject to the Seller approving the terms and the results of the valuation undertaken by the Buyer's Valuer pursuant to special condition 1, failing which the Seller may terminate this Contract. In that event the deposit is to be refunded to the Buyer, this matter will be at an end and neither party will have any claim against the other apart from a claim based on a breach of the Contract prior to the date of termination. The Buyer will give to the Seller a copy of the valuation within three working days of receiving it and the parties must advise each other within three working days of the date that the Buyer gives the Seller a copy of such valuation and whether the amount of the valuation and its terms are approved by them respectively under this clause and clause 1 above."

After digesting these clauses, readers will now be as surprised as me to know that there are sellers who will actually agree to sell their property at valuation less 10 per cent.

And who are these sellers? They're developers who can't move their stock and are prepared to sell to people who are willing to buy in blocks of, say, six or ten units at a time. A developer might agree to this arrangement provided they don't get "worked over" by a buyer and their valuer, because if they genuinely believe the valuation isn't realistic, the sellers don't have to proceed. The above clauses therefore allow for this process to occur and achieve the aims of the buyer and seller.

15 WHAT IS A BACK-UP CONTRACT AND WHEN CAN I USE IT?

Here's one recent example of the power of thinking creatively. A young client submitted her offer to buy a property and was advised by the agent that the seller had accepted an offer from another party.

She called to lament this fact to me and let me know that she was moving on to try to find another investment. "Don't be too quick to do that," I said. "See what you can find out about the terms of that contract (the price and any conditional clauses) and try to get a handle on the prospects of that contract proceeding to settlement." She was delighted to ring me the next day to inform me that her favourite agent had told her that the two gentlemen who had contracted to purchase the property had submitted offers through that agent for a lesser purchase price on two other properties, subject to finance, and on both occasions they failed to obtain approval of finance to proceed with the deal. The friendly agent was therefore very doubtful about the first buyer's ability to settle the purchase. Armed with this information, I suggested to my client that she submit a back-up contract to the seller, including a special clause which said that if the first purchase didn't proceed to settlement, then the property was hers.

From the seller's perspective they had nothing to lose in signing a back-up contract as it only gave them greater security. The clause that was ultimately used was similar to the following:

"The Seller warrants that the property is presently the subject of a Contract of Sale dated (complete) between themselves and (complete) as Buyer and that this contract is conditional upon the following matters:

A. approval of finance within 14 days from the date of that contract; and

B. a pest and building inspection of the property being to the satisfaction of the Buyer within 14 days from the date of that contract.

If any of the above conditions are not satisfied or waived in writing by the dates outlined above, the Seller must terminate such Contract.

This Contract is subject to the Buyer of the Contract referred to above, or the Seller, terminating that contract on or before 5pm on the (insert date), 20(complete). The Seller must not grant any extensions of time to the Buyer referred to above to allow the Buyer further time to obtain the approval of finance or satisfy itself in relation to the pest and building reports. The Seller also agrees not to vary the other terms of the Contract of Sale."

16 A BUYER OF MY PROPERTY WANTS TO PURCHASE SUBJECT TO AN INSPECTION – WHAT DO YOU THINK?

My client had been marketing her property for sale for a short period of time only when an offer to buy came in for the full asking price, subject to one small matter, or so my client thought. The "small matter" was "Subject to a physical inspection of the property by the buyer within 14 days." The buyer was from interstate and, although familiar with the area, did not know this specific property. The agent said that full plans, photos of the property and the surrounding homes and the streets had been sent to the buyer, so I didn't see any real problem with agreeing with this clause. It should have just been a "rubber stamp" approving the property in a fortnight's time when the buyer next visited the area.

"As a seller", I said, "Never agree to such a clause". My overwhelming experience with these clauses is that after the inspection the buyer always finds objections with the property and then uses this to try and lever down the price. I advised my client to reject the offer and direct her agent to advise the buyer that they should bring forward their visit to see the property as soon as possible and once they were impressed with how good it was, they could then make a strong cash offer. The property therefore would not be tied up to one potential buyer only during the 14-day inspection period and the seller would be free to accept other offers.

17 OFFERS BEFORE AUCTION – SHOULD I MAKE ONE?

A regular dilemma facing the many thousands of Australians who auction properties each year is this: what to do if an offer that comes close to the price the seller wants is made in the week or so before the auction. The agent asks you whether you want the buyers to submit the offer in writing so you can try to work them up to the price you're after. The danger and the dilemma for the seller is that in doing this it could be that the buyers don't come to the price you want, the offer is rejected and then they don't attend the auction because they feel it's a waste of time.

Another negative of this approach is that in the process of negotiating through written contracts before the auction you end up disclosing to the agent your auction reserve price. (It is almost a golden rule that you never disclose your reserve price to the agent until just before the auction commences.)

I received a call recently from a client seeking guidance on exactly this situation. His potential buyer was the only person who had made an offer on the property with only a week to go till the auction. From my discussions with him and the agent, although there were other interested parties that would be at the auction, this buyer was likely to be the one who would pay the highest price for the property. On balance I suggested that it was best to reject the verbal offer and get the buyer to the auction. Through the auction process he would be more likely to pay the price that the seller was asking.

In my experience, the only exception to this strategy would be if there were other potential buyers at around the price that was being offered who would also be there at the auction. Therefore, if you lost this buyer through the pre-auction negotiation process there would still likely be others who would attend the auction. As for disclosing your reserve price to an agent before the auction, the only exception to this rule would be if you were dealing with an exceptional agent.

How do you know that you are dealing with an

exceptional agent? An exceptional agent would be someone who works exclusively in your area, is easily the dominant agent in that area and who has achieved that status because they regularly achieve record prices for properties on behalf of sellers.

You might disclose your reserve price to such an agent in the knowledge that they'll use that information for your benefit, rather than against you.

18 THE CLAUSE YOU PREPARED, ROB, WAS REJECTED BY THE SELLER – WHAT DO I DO NOW?

The other attribute a successful investor needs to acquire is to learn to bounce back and be self-correcting. Here's an example. An agitated and dissatisfied client called me to complain about a clause I had drafted which he had included in a contract to purchase a property, which went as follows:

> "The Seller will allow the Buyer access to the property before settlement at reasonable times and upon reasonable notice to allow the Buyer to take measurements and obtain quotes for renovations and building work which he proposes to carry out following settlement."

The seller rejected the clause outright and wouldn't sign the contract. The seller's complaint was that the clause was open-ended and allowed the buyer unlimited access at any time during the day or weekend. I recommended that the buyer re-submit the contract and the clause with this additional sentence:

"Access, however, will be limited to between the hours of 9am and 5pm Monday to Friday on a maximum of six occasions only and provided that the Buyer gives to the Seller a minimum of 48 hours' notice in writing that he requires such access."

The contract was signed with the new clause without any objection from the seller. This story also illustrates the fact that in this changing market it's the people who are the most flexible who win.

19 I AM DEALING WITH A TOWN PLANNER FROM A REGIONAL COUNCIL – DO YOU HAVE ANY PRACTICAL TIPS?

Frustrated with the lean pickings of suitable properties in the suburbs surrounding Brisbane, an investor decided to try his luck in some of the country areas in regions past Beaudesert. He was surprised to find that owners of properties in these areas were becoming more accustomed to approaches from city buyers and were playing hard to get.

He found that after a number of attempts to buy properties in this country town, subject to due diligence or development application approval, he was unsuccessful. He decided to take a more commercial approach and maximise his chances at securing the properties by offering to buy them on the basis of unconditional contracts.

This would necessitate him making enquiries with the town planners at the local council to assess his prospects of attaining the development approval (DA) later. He asked me whether I had any practical tips for him. I suggested he make a personal appointment to see the most senior town planner he could at the council, rather than make his enquiries over the phone.

In country areas a lot of decisions are made by the council officers (town planners) rather than the councillors and it was important, I told him, that he get the most reliable advice on the day. I suggested he say something like this: "I'm just a beginner and so that I don't misunderstand you or misquote you, do you mind if I make notes of our meeting?"

When the meeting finished, I suggested he say, "Now, I just want to check that I've got this right", and then read back the notes he'd taken to the town planner.

This simple procedure, I believe, reduces the risk of misinterpretation, or to put it politely, a "rubbery" interpretation by that officer later (or their manager) of what they've told you.

As I've said before, it isn't the macro skills in life that are the most important for investors, it's the micro skills.

Don't become a ruthless negotiator

If you become ruthless in your negotiations there will always be a day of payback. Let me share with you a story of an opportunistic buyer who signed a contract to buy a commercial property, subject to due diligence, which illustrates this powerful message.

The buyer's due diligence was exhaustive in the hope he would uncover something he could hang his hat on and use as a lever to force the seller to reduce the price of the property. And he was successful in his endeavours, because the seller reduced the price by $100,000.

After he'd "worked over" the seller in this way, the buyer called me to ask that I document the reduction in the purchase price by an exchange of letters with the other solicitor.

While I personally didn't like his negotiating style, it's my job to follow my client's instructions so I did that promptly, but to the deep resentment of the seller who was very annoyed at being treated this way.

And, oh yes, there was a "night of long knives".

Three days before settlement, the buyer's bank advised that it couldn't settle on the due date and requested an extension of settlement for another week. In Queensland, where time is of the essence, this puts the buyer at the complete mercy of the seller.

"Payback time," you say. "Poetic Justice," is the other cry I hear.

My personal favourite though is "live by the sword, die by the sword", if we're talking clichés.

The seller played it beautifully and got the $100,000 back by agreeing to extend the settlement date on the basis that the price was reinstated to the original figure.

Before we get all moralistic about it, I've handled many transactions where it was the seller – and not the buyer – who took advantage of the other's misfortune of not being able to settle on the due date and insisted that settlement would only be extended if the purchase price was increased.

So it's worth spending a little time to discuss a strategy of how to handle this situation if you should find yourself in it one day.

Picture this: there you are, relying on the pity of the seller, begging for an extension of settlement and if they don't grant it, you're in breach of the contract. The very least that will happen to you is that you'll lose your deposit, and probably a good investment opportunity.

The better way to handle it is this: have your solicitor make the request for the extension and explain personally to the seller's solicitors the reason for it – for example, your bank's internal problems. Have them also assure the seller's solicitor there are no other impediments to settlement in, say, a week's time and that all of your searches of the property are in order (which you should know by now as settlement is imminent).

Wait then for the seller's response. Don't offer to increase the price or even offer to pay penalty interest for the delayed settlement. Just wait for the seller's response.

Once you have that response, let's say that they do ask for the purchase price to be increased by $100,000, then at least you have that end of it capped. That is, it's not going to get any worse.

Your strategy should then be to counter-offer something that's more palatable to you. Instead of counter-offering to pay an increased purchase price, have your solicitor personally (not by letter, as the call has more impact than a faxed or emailed letter) advise the other solicitors, on your instructions of course, that you don't have the financial ability to make payment of any more money because you're borrowing the maximum you can from your lender.

Instead, you might offer to release the deposit to the seller now, rather than waiting until settlement. If this doesn't quite get you there and, let's say the deposit you've paid is only 5 per cent of the purchase price, offer from the money you would have otherwise paid on settlement to increase the deposit to 10 per cent and release that to the seller. Often this offer to release cash now will burn a hole in their pocket and will be acceptable.

I've found this strategy will often get you there. It's an outcome you can live with rather than paying a lot more money for the property. Sure, it's risky to release the deposit before settlement, but you're in a no-win situation anyway where you're in default and pleading for the seller's lenience.

Finally, never offend the seller-occupier

I would like to finish up this section with a story that might strike a chord with many of you as property investors.

After speaking with a group of real estate salespeople about negotiating, one of them approached me to express his dismay at an unexpected response to an offer he'd made to a client seller in an economically depressed area.

The property had been on the market for almost nine months. (The average listing period of a property for sale in this area before procuring a contract was four to five months.)

The property was listed for sale at $600,000 and the salesman submitted an unconditional cash offer of

$500,000 with settlement within 21 days, with advice from the buyer to the seller to "take it or leave it".

The seller's response was just as quick: he rejected the offer outright. The salesman followed through with the usual overtures and enquired of the seller what it would take to secure a contract. The seller refused point blank to deal with this buyer and told the salesman it was because he was hurt by the offer and had no intention of ever dealing with this buyer again.

The question from the salesman to me was, "Why won't the seller deal with me and this buyer? I mean, it was nothing personal; it was just business. It's just a matter of reaching a price so why don't they deal?"

I enquired more about the seller's circumstances and was told the property had been his home for more than 20 years. During that time, the seller had raised four children in the property and clearly had a great emotional attachment to it. No wonder he was insulted by the amount of the offer and the way it was presented to him.

I told the salesman that selling to this vendor wasn't primarily about price. It was far more about emotion and that was what he had misinterpreted and played so fundamentally wrong. This was a very sobering thought for him and clearly worthy of his serious consideration, as it drew a long silence. I then said, "This seller wasn't selling this property just for money."

I diplomatically explained to the salesman that this seller was like a father to the bride at his daughter's wedding. He has nurtured his newborn daughter for 25 years and was now passing his precious bundle of joy over to another man's care and love. He wanted to pass this house over in the same loving way, such was the emotional investment. No wonder he was greatly annoyed by this less than courteous approach by the buyer.

"What should I do now then?" the salesman asked.

"Absolutely nothing", I said. "Leave them alone and don't go near them. If in two or three months' time the property is still on the market you might then make an ever-so-gentle approach to the seller again to gauge his interest in selling to this buyer. But don't be surprised if you never get your foot back in the door again."

I recall a friend of mine who made the same classic mistake when offering to buy a commercial property from a Chinese group using the same style of negotiation. They, too, were so insulted they still refused to deal with my friend more than six months later.

> *"The Dalai Lama visited the White House and told the President that he could teach him to find a higher state of consciousness. Then, after talking to George W. Bush for a few minutes, he said "You know what? Let's just grab lunch instead."*
>
> JAY LENO, AMERICAN COMEDIAN

Part III
SMART QUESTIONS ABOUT FINANCE APPROVAL AND VENDOR FINANCE

If you owe the bank $1,000, that's your problem. If you owe the bank $100 million, that's the bank's problem.

J PAUL GETTY, AMERICAN BILLIONAIRE

Smart Questions about Finance Approval and Vendor Finance

With all of the legal jargon and the peppering of real estate contracts these days, real estate agents and investors are becoming more gun-shy about the use of special conditions in real estate contracts. They're pushing back in the marketplace when requests are made to include special clauses in contracts of sale, for whatever reason.

All too frequently, therefore, investors are encouraged to withdraw their requests for clauses or are offered an apparently simpler, more straightforward clause – prepared by the real estate agent – to replace the one prepared by, say, the investor's property lawyer.

I, however, take a different approach and like to educate my investor clients that a creative and intelligent use of special conditions can facilitate a transaction, not hinder it.

Use of street-smart and property-savvy clauses can allow you as an investor to take advantage of an opportunity that just wasn't there when you operated under a cloud of ignorance.

So listen up all you investors who have been duped by the mantra of the real estate agents who tell you, "Less is yes". That is, the fewer clauses there are in your offer, the greater chance you have of getting a "Yes" from the seller. Add the story that follows as a resource to what should be an ever-growing collection of anecdotes and pearls of wisdom that you are collecting as in investor and start looking at the use of clauses in real estate contracts through these new eyes of perception. Picture yourself now in the scenario outlined in Question 20.

> *"When I was a kid, my parents moved a lot. But I always found them."*
>
> TONY LENAN, SOLICITOR

20 MY OFFER IS $40K LESS THAN THE SELLER IS ASKING. ANY TIPS FOR BRIDGING THE GAP?

After much diligent research, you finally find yourself looking at a property that meets all your selection criteria. The sellers, though, aren't negotiable on the price and if you want to do this deal you'll have to pay that price. You do your sums and after you inject all of your own cash and borrow the maximum amount your lender will allow, you're still $40,000 short of the asking price.

Here's the scenario:

Purchase price	$450,000
Your cash injection	$90,000
Balance	$360,000
Less maximum loan	$320,000
Shortfall	$40,000

When you realise there'll be a shortfall, your first reaction is, "Perhaps I should have a look at a cheaper property", or worse still, "I should try to save up the extra $40,000". You decide instead to call your solicitor and ask, "How can I buy this property without putting any more money down?" Your solicitor suggests: "Why not offer to buy the property on the basis of a $40,000 loan from the sellers?" During conversations you've had with the sellers over several inspections of the property, you're aware that they're planning to move into a retirement village nearby, where they've already secured a unit. From comments made by the real estate agent you're also aware that this property is only going to cost them $350,000 and they're going to invest the balance of $100,000 into a cash management account, which you know will carry an interest rate of about 5 per cent per annum.

Armed with this knowledge, herein lies an opportunity. My suggestion to you is to tell the sellers you'll pay their asking price without any quibbling if they'll lend you the shortfall of $40,000, at 5 per cent per annum for, say, 12 months on the security of a second mortgage over the property (your own lender will be taking a first mortgage as security for the loan of $320,000). You tell them that over the next year you'll make some improvements to the property and following that you expect to get the property re-valued, at which time you'll have additional funds to repay the loan. Will the seller have any problem with the property offered as security for this loan of $40,000? Of course not – it's their own home.

If the proposal is properly explained to them, it's a low-risk proposal from their perspective. After all, you have substantial equity in the property of $90,000 and they will hold a registered second mortgage as security for their loan. If the sellers have some reservations about your proposal, why not offer to pay them an interest rate of 10 per cent per annum (that's double what they'd otherwise get in the cash management account).

Too many people have tunnel vision when they get to this stage of negotiations and baulk at paying twice the interest rate that the sellers would get from a financial institution. Look at the big picture here. This will only add an additional $2,000 to the transaction and will get you the property. If you need to, why not make your offer so sweet to the sellers that it's irresistible. Offer to "capitalise" the 10 per cent interest by showing the loan amount as

$44,000 (the vendor loan of $40,000 plus $4,000 interest) with the documentation to show no interest payable. In this way the couple will receive the return of loan monies and the interest in one year's time, tax-free. The "interest" now gets added onto the purchase price so that the deal looks like this:

Purchase price	$454,000
Your cash injection	$90,000
Balance	$364,000
Advance from your lender	$320,000
Shortfall	$44,000

A sample of a clause that could be used is the following:

> "The Seller will lend to the Buyer on settlement $44,000 to assist the Buyer to finance the purchase of the property on the security of a registered second mortgage over the property on the following terms:
>
> Term: 1 year from the date of completion
> Interest rate: nil
>
> All costs and expenses (including stamp duty and reasonable professional legal costs) involved in the negation, preparation, stamping and registration of the mortgage documents to be paid by the Buyer.
>
> The amount of the first mortgage will be limited to a principal sum of $320,000 plus any charges and expenses. The Buyer will arrange for the first mortgagee of the property to enter into a Deed of Priority prepared by the Seller's solicitors at the Buyer's cost (those costs to be reasonable) on usual and reasonable terms, on or before the completion date, limiting the amount of its first mortgage to that principal sum, charges and expenses.
>
> The Buyer's obligation to arrange for the first mortgagee to enter into the Deed of Priority on or before completion is a fundamental term of the Contract.

Early repayment – the Buyer will have the right to make early repayment of the whole of the loan only upon giving 30 days' notice in writing to the Seller of their intention to do so. All other terms of the mortgage will be reasonable and determined by the Seller's Solicitors.

The Seller's obligations under this clause are a fundamental term of this Contract."

By understanding and using the concept of vendor finance in this most simple way, I have illustrated to you the importance of educating yourself about these strategies. Knowledge really is power.

21 SECOND MORTGAGES – JUST HOW GOOD ARE THEY?

I took a call from a client who had been trying for some time to sell his property. Finally, he advised me that he had found someone who was prepared to meet his price of $700,000 but the buyer wanted him to finance part of the purchase price himself by "leaving in" $200,000 of the sale price for a period of nine months from settlement. During this time the buyer would pay 10 per cent interest (and on the security of a second registered mortgage over the property). "The question for you, Mr Solicitor", he said was, "What do you think about second mortgages as security for such a loan?"

My advice was that second mortgages are generally poor forms of security because you are the second cab off the rank. Everything that you do as the holder of a second mortgage when selling the property (in the case of default) is first and foremost for the benefit of the first mortgagee. Only after they have had the first bite of the cake and been repaid all of their monies, and only if there is something left over, do you receive anything. Mortgagee sales, too, have a perception in the marketplace of being distress sales and regularly attract buyers who make low-ball offers, thus leading to the real prospect of a shortfall in sale proceeds to pay out both the first and second mortgagee. It is crucial therefore, that there is a limit placed on the amount of the first mortgage so that your second mortgage had real value. The Contract of Sale would therefore need to include a clause along the following lines:

> "The Amount
>
> The amount of the first mortgage would be limited to a principal sum of $700,000.00 plus any charges and expenses. The Buyer will arrange for the first mortgagee of the property to enter into a Deed of Priority prepared by the Seller's solicitors at the Buyer's cost (those costs to be reasonable) on usual and reasonable terms, on or before completion date, limiting the amount of the first mortgage to that principal sum, charges and expenses.
>
> The Buyer's obligation to arrange for the first mortgagee to enter into the Deed of Priority on or before completion is a fundamental term of this Contract."

22 WOULD YOU USE VENDOR FINANCE TO SELL A SLOW-MOVING PROPERTY?

A softening real estate market prompted a client to look for suggestions about how to market and sell a property that had proved difficult to move. Her question was, "What do you think about offering vendor finance to a prospective purchaser for, say, 10 per cent of the purchase price?"

She'd received a number of calls from interested buyers who'd only had a minimum deposit of 5 to 10 per cent of the asking price. Their lenders would advance 80 to 90 per cent of the price but they were still short 10 per cent because of stamp duty and legal costs.

If you are considering vendor finance as a seller, you should appreciate that your buyer will grant a first mortgage to another lender and that your security for your loan will be a second mortgage. For a second mortgage to have any real value, there must be a limit placed on the amount of the principal sum secured by the first mortgage. It's therefore essential your contract of sale contains a provision that requires your buyer to obtain from their lender (the first mortgagee) what is called a Deed of Priority. This limits the amount for which the first lender takes priority over your loan. Without a Deed of Priority, your second mortgage could end up worthless.

Another tip is to ensure your contract of sale provides that your purchaser gives your consent under the *Privacy Act* to conduct a credit check of their financial history, or at least provide you with a copy of their own credit check which they can obtain themselves. There's no point offloading a property with the help of vendor finance only to find out down the track that your buyer is a serial defaulter and you never end up getting the repayment of your loan. Another good idea is to ensure the vendor finance is for as short a period as possible (ideally under one year) so there's maximum pressure on the buyer to repay your loan. You'll usually be dealing with the bottom end of the market in this scenario so be sure to protect yourself.

23 MORTGAGE PROTECTION INSURANCE – WHAT DO YOU THINK ABOUT THIS WAY OF GETTING AROUND IT?

My second call for the year came from another parent trying to give their son a leg-up in buying his first piece of real estate. His mother complained to me about all of the costs and charges incurred in buying real estate which can create a real barrier to entry for a first-time buyer, especially the cost of mortgage protection insurance (a one-off fee paid to a mortgage insurer where the borrower has a low equity – less than 20 per cent of the purchase price). Lenders require the security of a mortgage protection policy as it guarantees payment of their loan if the borrower defaults. The cost will often be more than 2 per cent of the amount of the loan.

A typical example I saw last year was on a loan of $500,000 and the cost of procuring the mortgage protection insurance came to more than $11,000. My client said she'd read about a way to get around this insurance. A number of big banks were suggesting a way to avoid this fee was for parents to go part-guarantor for the loan. That is, they guaranteed the top 20 per cent of the amount of the loan, in much the same way, she thought, as when a parent guaranteed the loan for their youngster to purchase their first car. It is, however, a lot more serious than that, I explained. For a start there are additional loan application fees and guarantor's fees payable to the bank on this arrangement. More importantly, the bank requires the parents to not only guarantee part of the loan but also put up their home as security for the kid's loan and the parents' guarantee.

Most of the banks want a first mortgage from the parents, which means the parents must have paid off their home loan first. Another client of mine obtained a costing from their bank on this type of arrangement recently where they were borrowing $450,000 from their bank. It was proposed that her parents guarantee part of the loan and put up their home as security for this guarantee. When my client added up all the costs of this arrangement, including application fee, guarantor's fee and the cost of obtaining a valuation over her parents' house, the bill came to more than $3,000. So when this proposal is examined carefully it's easy to see that the savings of the mortgage protection fee are partly offset by the imposition of some additional fees and the locking-in of the parents' property to the lender. But this will have serious consequences if the parents want to sell later or take a line of credit over their property to finance other real estate dealings themselves.

I prefer lending your child the extra money to avoid the need for mortgage protection insurance, rather than the above arrangement. But if you do that, don't forget to get a signed loan agreement from your offspring (and even a second mortgage over your child's home if you want full protection) for these monies, so that repayment of your loan is protected in case your loan is claimed to be a gift by your child's spouse in the future (if they end up in the family court down the track). Let's face it, this is a real risk as almost 50 per cent of first marriages end up in divorce. If you paid the insurance fee yourself to get your child into the property, everyone is better off.

24 DOES A FINANCE CLAUSE IN A CONTRACT REALLY ALLOW THE BUYER TO JUST 'WALK AWAY' IF THEY HAVE A CHANGE OF HEART?

It's a common misconception that a "subject to finance" clause allows a buyer to simply withdraw from a transaction because they've had a change of heart about the purchase (for example, they believe it's not a fruitful bargain), on the pretence that they couldn't secure the loan.

A very cynical client of mine had been caught one time too many by such a buyer (the last three sales of his home had fallen through because of alleged non-approval of finance). When he attempted to challenge the genuineness of the claim by the buyer on the last and second last occasion, the agent advised him that he had no right to do so unless he took the matter all the way through the court process. I suggested, therefore, that he include the following simple clause in future contracts, which moved the power on this issue from the buyer to him as a seller:

> "Regardless of any other clause in this Contract the Buyer will not be entitled to terminate this Contract on the grounds that finance was not approved, or not approved on terms satisfactory to the Buyer, unless the buyer produces evidence

in writing from a lender or finance broker that an application was made to the lender for finance and the lender made a decision in relation to such application."

I was recently on the other end of an unsettling telephone call from a frustrated seller. He had fallen victim one time too many to the ultimate "escape clause". He had just lost a contract on the sale of his house because the buyers advised they had not obtained finance approval on terms satisfactory to them (the standard provision in contracts throughout every state in Australia).

He had heard on the grapevine from another local real estate agent in the area that the buyer had simply got cold feet on the sale and decided to terminate the contract on the supposed basis of finance not being approved. Like someone scorned by an ex-lover, he wanted justice.

"As a matter of principle," my client exclaimed, "I am not going to let this lie". Offended and deeply suspicious that the buyer was just not acting in good faith (an implied term in every real estate contract) he asked me whether he could freeze the release of the deposit to the buyer until they proved that they had made a genuine application to a lender and had been rejected (or the conditions of approval were unreasonably onerous to a buyer). "No, he could not," was my advice. "The reality is", I advised him, "that under standard finance clauses a buyer has no obligation to produce evidence that they have made an application for finance and reveal the outcome of this application. The position would have been different, I advised, if his contract had included the following special condition:

"Should this Contract be subject to finance and such application be declined by the financier or approved on terms not satisfactory to the Buyer, further to the terms and conditions of this Contract, the Buyer agrees to provide a copy of the relevant correspondence from the financier to the Seller's solicitor. Until such a copy of correspondence from the financier is received by the Seller/s solicitor, the Seller/s shall be under no obligation to refund the deposit monies to the Buyer".

As security that the buyer will always honour their obligation to act in good faith, and provide the evidence set out in the special condition above (in the event that they seek to escape from a contract on the basis that finance has not been approved on terms satisfactory to them), I suggested that he insist that a substantial deposit always be paid by a buyer on the signing of a contract. If my client's buyer had put down say $30,000 as a deposit (rather than the common token initial deposit of $1,000 or $2,000) he might have acted very differently if there was any prospect of him not getting back his sizeable deposit, because he had not complied with the express or implied terms in the contract of sale.

25 THE FINANCE APPROVAL FROM THE BROKER WAS SEVEN PAGES LONG. HOW DO I KNOW IF FINANCE IS REALLY APPROVED?

A beginner investor engaged my services to handle the purchase of her first residential investment property. The contract was subject to a loan approval for $500,000 within 21 days from the date of the contract. After 21 days, the investor was advised that it would be a few more days before an approval letter was forthcoming. I requested an extension of the finance date for a few extra days to accommodate this delay and the seller grudgingly agreed to grant the extension. A few days later, a very short finance approval letter was issued by the lender, advising that finance for $500,000 had been approved for a term of 10 years at an attractive interest rate. The letter went on to state that the full terms of the letter of approval would be sent some time in the next week.

My client rang me with the "finance approval" letter in her hand and asked me to sign off on the finance approval and go unconditional. I strongly cautioned her against this and advised her that the letter she'd obtained wasn't complete enough for her to make a commercial decision about whether to accept the loan offer as it didn't contain a full set of terms and conditions.

She asked, "What else could there be more important than the amount, the interest rate and the term?" Coincidently, I had on my desk a full approval letter for a $500,000 loan for another investor setting out the complete set of terms and I ran my beginner investor client through some of the matters that weren't dealt with in her brief letter. These included the following:

- **Mortgage protection insurance.** A condition that she take out mortgage protection insurance, as the loan amount was more than 80 per cent of the purchase price of the property. This protected the insurer should the borrower ever be unable to pay the loan, and the cost of that was $14,500.
- **Subject to valuation of the property.** If the valuation

didn't meet or better the purchase price, then the lender would only lend 90 per cent of the valuation and not the purchase price. Where does the shortfall come from?

- **Deferred application fee.** The lender imposed an application fee of $6,000 but deferred it provided that the borrower kept the loan for a minimum of five years. If the loan was only held for four years, eleven months and two weeks and paid out because of the sale of the property, then the full $6,000 deferred application fee would be payable by the borrower.

- **Payout of other loan.** It's common for lenders to require payout of personal loans and car loans as a condition of approving an investment loan where the borrower's capacity to pay is borderline or they're borrowing a high percentage of the purchase price.

My client was startled by the possibility of a lender imposing any or all of these conditions and made a hurried phone call to the broker. The broker confirmed her fears when he told her that the letter she received was simply a "congratulations letter" and that a full letter setting out all the conditions was still to come. The broker also advised her that he expected the conditions to include all of the conditions I had pointed out to her.

The beginner investor was now faced with a dilemma. Should she ask for another extension of a week to wait for the full approval letter? The risk that she ran in doing that was that the seller might not grant the extension and terminate the contract, and she would lose the deal. Alternatively she could "go unconditional" and take the risk that there was nothing nasty that she couldn't deal with in the final approval letter. I strongly suggested she seek the extension and run the risk of losing the deal rather than the alternative. Another good deal would come along if she lost this one.

Finance Clauses – from a Seller's Perspective

My first call of the week came from a client who had signed a contract of sale as a seller four days earlier, subject to the buyer obtaining finance approval. The agent then rang her on a Sunday afternoon to say that the buyer had just called her and given her the heads up that she wasn't going to make the grade with her finance application and the deal was going to fall over. So, the question for me was, "Can I, as the seller, now terminate this contract and enter into a new one with another keen buyer who has just appeared on the scene in the last 24 hours? I want to move quickly and not lose them."

My response was simple, "No, you can't". The reason being that finance clauses are for the buyer's benefit *exclusively*. The buyer has the property tied up for another 10 days and can string you along for that period before advising you that finance isn't approved.

The question was another critical reminder that finance clauses should be kept as short as possible from a seller's perspective and any extensions of the dates that are granted should be for the shortest periods possible. As a seller you need to be on top of your game and grant requests for extensions for the finance approval period for as short a period as possible to keep the tightest possible leash on the buyer.

At the end of the day, you should know that finance

clauses are almost the best escape clause possible for buyers looking to extricate themselves from an unfruitful bargain. My best advice to the caller was, armed with this advice from the agent we should immediately write to the buyer's solicitor and invite them to terminate the contract of sale in view of this development. Hopefully, this would prompt confirmation earlier rather than later that the sale won't be proceeding and allow the seller to enter into the second contract. Only then is it safe to enter into another contract of sale.

The Negatives of Equity-based Loans

Equity-based loans are loans that are linked or capped to the amount of equity you have in a property.

A typical condition in such loans requires the property to be revalued every, say, two years.

I'm seeing a real emergence of loan approvals from lenders with this as a standard condition today.

If the valuation commissioned by the bank two years out from when you took out the loan shows a drop in the value of the property by, say, 10 per cent, then the bank will require you to inject further equity into the property, or repay the loan. It won't matter that you're up to date with your mortgage payments and haven't missed a beat in any of these payments over the past two years.

Such loan conditions don't serve you at all as they aren't related to your ability to pay, your credit history over the past two years or your repayment history over that time. Also, when these clauses kick in they usually do so at a time when you can least afford it, and your ability to arrange a refinance through another lender could be seriously impaired because of the fall in the market. You've been entrapped!

Any reservations about the feeling that you're now being savaged while you're down will be put beyond any doubt when you receive the account for the valuation (yes, payable by you under the loan agreement you signed two years ago).

Such conditions calculatingly position the bank to take advantage of you with no benefit to you at all. I therefore recommend that you reject these clauses and fight hard to insist the bank removes them or you'll find yourself another lender.

This valuation condition is just an opportunistic way for the bank to improve its position after the event. It was more than happy two years ago to tip this money into your wallet, but now two years later it may require you to inject a further 10 per cent equity. This is just not fair at all to you as a borrower.

> *"It's not true that I had nothing on. I had the radio on."*
> MARILYN MONROE, SEX SYMBOL

Part IV
SMART QUESTIONS ABOUT UNITS AND BODY CORPORATES

She got her looks from her father. He is a plastic surgeon.

GROUCHO MARX, AMERICAN COMEDIAN

Smart Questions About Units and Body Corporates

Property investment is a bittersweet mixture of success and mistakes. As an investor you have triumphs and victories, as well as misadventures and mishaps. Nowhere are these statements more apt than in the area of investment in strata title units involving a body corporate structure. I am regularly asked which is the area where Australians make the most mistakes in property investment and it is without doubt in the area of purchase of strata title units.

But you will make mistakes as a property investor regardless of the area in which you invest, or your strategy. The antidote for mistakes is, however, education. Education will protect you against the cruel vicissitudes and the harsh side of the world of property and be more forgiving of the human frailty and propensity to make mistakes.

So keep up your education about this area of the marketplace. Let me do my bit in continuing that education by sharing with you some of the more frequently asked questions about unit purchase and ownership.

> *"Never marry for money. Divorce for money."*
> WENDY LIEBMAN, AMERICAN COMEDIAN

26 I AM BUYING A UNIT IN A SMALL BLOCK OF THREE UNITS AND I AM TOLD THAT THERE IS NO BODY CORPORATE. IS THIS AN ISSUE?

There are countless duplexes and triplexes across the country where, after registration of the body corporate or strata scheme, the owners let the operation of the body corporate lapse. They simply agree amongst themselves about who is responsible for maintenance and mowing the lawns and which insurance company they'll jointly appoint to insure the building.

This makes sense from a practical point of view, although the dilemma for you is that once the body corporate has been established – which must occur to allow separate title deeds to be issued for the units – the owners of those units and future owners have a legal obligation to maintain the operation of that body corporate.

How can you be sure then, as the purchaser of a duplex or a triplex, that things are as simple as they appear?

If you purchase a unit in a strata title scheme, where the body corporate is operational, you can protect yourself by making the contract subject to a search of the body corporate records and you being satisfied with the results of this search. The results of this search will reveal one way or another whether everything is good on the home front or not. However, if the body corporate has been inactive for many years, carrying out a search will be pointless. You can still, of course, search the Titles Office's records to confirm what by-laws apply to the body corporate and find out the location of any common property and any exclusive-use areas, but that will reveal nothing about the operation of the body corporate.

The way to bridge the gap in these circumstances is to physically meet with your neighbours in the complex to satisfy yourself that there's nothing untoward going on. This is a must. It's the only real way to obtain the peace of mind you need to be satisfied that the fact the body corporate has never conducted annual general meetings or struck any levies doesn't come back to haunt you down the track.

A sample of the clause I recommend be added to every unit purchase contract is the following:

> "This Contract is subject to the Buyer undertaking an inspection of the Body Corporate records and being satisfied with the outcome of this inspection within fourteen (14) days from the date of this Contract, failing which the Buyer will be entitled to terminate this Contract and in that event the deposit will be refunded to the Buyer and neither party will have any claim against the other."

Body corporate liability

A client consulted me recently about a purchase of a unit where the vendor was more than honest with her and disclosed that there was an action between a guest of the building who had injured herself when a large metal garbage bin on rollers, that hadn't been properly secured by the resident manager, accidentally rolled down the hill into her causing her serious injuries. The body corporate insurer disclaimed liability for the accident and placed responsibility for it squarely at the foot of the manager who wasn't insured. There was serious doubt whether the body corporate or the manager was liable, and if the body corporate was liable its insurer maintained that it wasn't covered by its policy of insurance.

If the body corporate was held responsible for the injuries, then a substantial award would have been imposed upon it which would have resulted in the raising of special levies against each and every owner of at least $5,000 to $10,000 each. Monies were held back in a trust account following settlement to cover this contingency because we added the following clause to the contract of sale to protect her position:

> "The Parties acknowledge that a former tenant of a unit of the complex has brought a claim against the Body Corporate for personal injuries arising out of an accident in the complex. The Sellers agree to indemnify the Buyer in respect of any liability suffered by the Buyer as a lot owner in the respect of this claim and in particular without limitation, any levies struck by the Body Corporate to pay for this claim.
>
> As security for any such liability the Seller agrees that $10,000 of the purchase price payable on settlement will be retained by the Buyer's solicitors in trust until the proceedings based on this claim are settled, discontinued or are determined by a court of law.
>
> In the event of a dispute about payment from the monies held in trust under this clause or any other matter relating to this clause, such dispute shall be referred to a solicitor appointed by the president of the Queensland Law Society for their determination and such solicitor shall act as an expert and not as an arbitrator and their decision shall be final and binding on the parties".

27 DO I NEED TO GET BODY CORPORATE APPROVAL TO KEEP MY CAT IN THIS UNIT THAT I AM BUYING?

A couple of "empty-nester" clients called to advise that they'd decided to downsize. They'd sold their house and now wished to sign a contract to buy a small townhouse. The question they had for me was whether they needed to make their contract to buy the townhouse subject to the body corporate's approval to keep their pedigree, and much spoilt, Siamese cat. They said they'd thought twice before ringing me because they assumed they'd have the right to keep a small domestic cat in their new property but they decided they'd better confirm this assumption out of abundance of caution. Good thing they did, because the harsh reality with bodies corporate is that there are often severe restrictions on keeping animals within units and in many complexes there's a total prohibition on doing so. This is because when people live in such close confines to others, what might be your "darling" could end up being someone else's "nightmare".

I told the callers about an incident where one of my other clients tried to sneak a domestic cat into their unit after settlement, only to be met with strong resistance from the body corporate committee which immediately advised her that pets were illegal in the complex.

She then made an application to the Commissioner for Community Titles for permission to keep the cat, as she believed it had little impact on the residential amenity of the other owners in the complex. Although she was successful in getting permission to keep the cat, the conflict and disharmony that was generated from her keeping the cat in this complex, against the wishes of the other owners, eventually resulted in her selling the unit and moving on. If only she had made enquiries about this matter before she signed the contract, or at least made the contract subject to satisfying herself she could get approval to keep the cat, she could have avoided the whole unsavoury and expensive experience. An appropriate clause to use is the following:

> "Approval of family pet
>
> This Contract is subject to the buyer obtaining the Body Corporate's approval to keep their pedigree Siamese cat on the Scheme and in the lot within 21 days from the date of this Contract on terms satisfactory to them, failing which they will be entitled to terminate this Contract and in that event this matter will be at an end, the deposit refunded to the Buyer and neither party will have a claim against the other apart from any rights either of the parties will have against the other as a result of any breach of this Contract prior to termination.
>
> This clause has been inserted for the benefit of the Buyer and may be waived by notice in writing to the Seller at any time before settlement."

28 HOW DO I MAKE SURE THAT ALL FORWARD BOOKINGS OF MY HOLIDAY UNIT I HAVE JUST SOLD ARE PASSED ON TO THE BUYER?

I received a call from a client who'd sold one of her units in Surfers Paradise and made the most common mistake in the book when it comes to selling units. That is, she failed to pass on to the buyer of the unit the benefit/burden of forward bookings made by the resident manager or the letting agent. The law is very clear and provides that forward bookings made by an owner of a unit or by their agent is binding upon that owner and if the buyer of the unit fails to honour those bookings then the seller can be sued for the loss and damage that flows to the tenant (and this will often be considerable, as the unit would usually have been booked for holiday purposes). Imagine the sympathy a magistrate would have in a claim brought by an upset guest whose holiday had been ruined because the unit that they booked a year earlier for their holidays had been sold and the buyer wouldn't honour the forward booking because they wanted to use the property themselves. The way to avoid such a problem is to insert the following clause in the contract of sale:

> "The Buyer acknowledges that the lot purchased is subject to future tenancies which may have been arranged as casual holiday tenancies by the Seller's letting agent and the Buyer agrees to accept possession subject to such tenancies."

29 HOW DO I DEAL WITH A REAL TROUBLE-MAKER IN MY BODY CORPORATE WHEN I AM SELLING?

I was once asked by an investor, "I'm selling my unit to move into my first home. My second child has now arrived and we have outgrown unit living. It's a unit in a block of

60, mainly filled with young couples starting off their lives together, except for one cranky old widower who complains about everything. He regularly lodges applications to the Tribunal (the independent umpire that resolves disputes between unit owners in strata complexes), disputing how the body corporate spends its money. What concerns me is his latest application for the body corporate to raise a special levy of $4,000 per unit to fund a $250,000 expense to upgrade the lift. The body corporate manager advises this upgrade isn't necessary for many years yet. Nonetheless, this man is continuing with his application to the Tribunal. Do we have to disclose this unfounded claim to any buyer of our unit, and if they get anxious about it despite what we tell them, how do we overcome this objection to achieve the sale?"

My answer was, "Yes, you must disclose it".

This application constitutes a contingent liability of the body corporate that, if he is successful, wouldn't be payable as part of the regular operating expenses of the body corporate. It can also be legally regarded as an action that affects the property, or part of it, under most standard contracts and therefore should be revealed to the buyer. That being the case, it's best to raise it with the buyer.

The solution to resolving any buyer anxiety on this issue is to advise them that you accept responsibility for any negative financial outcome of this man's application. Do it by adding a special condition to the contract of sale.

The investor responded by saying, "My agent has told me not to worry about it. She said that I don't have to disclose it as these sorts of things are common in body corporates. She says it's a case of 'buyer beware' and I shouldn't go making things hard for myself by disclosing it as you've suggested."

My feedback to that comment was, "Such ignorant comments are usually the prelude to a big investor mistake. My advice is to disclose it".

Here's the clause I suggested she add to the contract:

> "The Buyer acknowledges that an owner in a complex has filed an application before the Body Corporate and Community Management Tribunal requesting orders that the Body Corporate strike a special levy upon all owners to fund the cost of improving/upgrading the lift for the complex at a cost of $250,000.
>
> The Sellers will make payment of any additional levies struck by the Body Corporate because of any orders made by the Tribunal regarding this matter where there are insufficient monies in the Body Corporate's sinking fund to be collected by the Body Corporate under its future sinking fund forecast to cover such payment.
>
> As Security for the vendor's obligations under this clause, the vendor will deposit $6,000 of the proceeds of sale on settlement in their solicitor's trust account to be held by their solicitor in trust for the period of one year from the date of settlement. The vendors authorise their solicitors to make payment from such monies to compensate the buyer for such additional levies and, at the end of the period of one year from the date of settlement, to make payment of the balance of the monies in trust (if any) to the vendors.
>
> The vendors' liability in relation to this matter will be limited to the monies held in trust and any dispute between the parties about whether monies are payable may be referred at the request of either party to a solicitor to be appointed by the president for the time being of the

Queensland Law Society, with the cost of such referral to be made from monies held in trust and if such funds are insufficient, to be shared equally between the parties. Such solicitor shall act as expert and their decision shall be final and binding upon the parties."

> *"But enough about me. Let's talk about you. What do you think of me?"*
>
> BETTE MIDLER, AMERICAN SINGER AND ACTOR

Part V
SMART QUESTIONS ABOUT BUYING UNITS OFF THE PLAN

I spent a lot of my money on booze, birds and fast cars – the rest I just squandered.

GEORGE BEST, FOOTBALLER

Smart Questions About Buying Units Off the Plan

Throughout this book, I promote a philosophy that you should as an investor become the best generalist that you possibly can be, that is, learn as much as you can generally about property law, negotiating, town planning and taxation. As an investor you will be confronted with issues that will require solutions and having an attitude of becoming generally aware about as many of these things as you can will serve you well in dealing with these issues and coming up with the solutions.

The benefit of this philosophy is very apparent when you look at the area of buying units off the plan. These purchases are now commonplace in Australia (and it is worth reminding yourself that almost every unit in the country was at some stage sold to someone "off the plan") and yet it is an area where investors seem to operate under the principle that ignorance is bliss. They accept Contracts of Sale produced to them by developers that are heavily weighted against them. And why do they do that? It is the lure of buying off the plan and the enticement of capital gains. In a nutshell, it is buying a property at today's price and paying for it tomorrow. But this enticement can turn sour unless you are educated.

As the purchaser of a unit off the plan when issues arise you will need to be like an archer. You will need to draw an arrow out of your quiver that you have on your back, load your bow and fire straight and true and if successful you will solve the problem. The issue is, though, that you need to have as many arrows in your quiver as possible. That is, have as much general knowledge and education as possible so you have the arrows to load up your bow to come up with the solutions. So here it is, "Buying units of the plan 101" which I will deal with in my usual style by sharing with you questions that have come across my desk as a practising solicitor.

> *"Too bad all the people who know how to run the country are busy driving cabs and cutting hair."*
>
> GEORGE BURNS, AMERICAN COMEDIAN

30 AM I PROTECTED AGAINST BUILDING DEFECTS WHEN I BUY OFF THE PLAN?

Buying units off the plan has become so commonplace in Australia that it is essential that investors and their advisers are aware of the many hidden pitfalls and traps. As investors who are buying off the plan are purchasing something that has not yet been built they need to be certain they minimise surprises when they come to take possession of the property. More importantly, they need to be sure that they are completely happy with the property when it is completed and it's time to make the final payment.

A client asked me for advice about a clause in a contract to buy a $400,000 unit off the plan. The clause stated that she, as the buyer, acknowledged that she had no right to inspect the unit before settlement, however the developer agreed to remedy any building defects that were brought to his attention within three months of settlement.

My advice was that I wouldn't part with $400,000 of my money for something I couldn't see until after I'd paid. I suggested she replace the clause with the following:

> "The Buyer will be entitled to inspect the unit not later than one week before settlement and the Buyer will be entitled to advise the Seller at that time of any defects, shrinkages or other faults due to faulty materials or workmanship in the construction of the lot and its fixtures, fittings, furnishings and chattels. In the event that the Buyer advises the Seller of any such matters, the Seller will at its expense and in a good

> and workmanlike manner rectify such defects, shrinkages or faults to the Buyer's satisfaction before settlement and this contract is subject to the Seller making such rectifications by settlement, failing which the Buyer will be entitled to terminate this contract. In that event this matter will be at an end, the deposit refunded to the Buyer and neither party will have a claim against the other apart from any rights either of the parties will have against the other as a result of any breach of contract prior to termination.
>
> This clause has been inserted for the benefit of the Buyer and may be waived by notice in writing to the Seller at any time before settlement."

The same client returned to me a week later and advised that the developer had agreed to insert the clause set out above (so much for the salesman's claim to my client that the developer wouldn't agree to any changes to his documentation – a common bluff).

She said the developer had also agreed to do some extra work to her unit and asked me to draft a clause to be included in the contract that required him to do so before settlement. I suggested the following clause:

> "The Seller agrees at its expense to carry out the following works and fit the following additional items using quality materials and in a good and workmanlike manner by settlement and its obligation to do so is a fundamental term of this contract." (Insert details of works to be carried out here).
>
> This clause has been inserted for the benefit of the Buyer and may be waived by notice in writing to the Seller at any time before settlement."

31 UNDER WHAT CIRCUMSTANCES CAN I DELAY SETTLEMENT?

Common sales documentation used by developers provides that you have no right to delay settlement or withhold money if the unit is unfit to occupy, contains building defects or is simply filthy. Developers' documentation usually provides that the developer will attend to these matters within three months of settlement. What do you do, then, if you find yourself in a similar position to a client of mine last year? She was crying in her beer about a unit which she had to settle that week. She'd borrowed heavily to buy the unit but the unit was nowhere near ready to rent out. It would be weeks or even a month or two before the developer put the unit in a fit state to rent out. Until that happened, they had no rental income to pay their mortgage payments. If only they'd included a clause like the one below in the contract of sale:

> "A. The Vendor warrants that the lot and the scheme and all facilities within the scheme will be in a clean and tidy condition on the date of completion and available and fit for use and occupation by the purchaser or its tenant and, in particular and without limitation, the lot and carpets will be professionally cleaned and all building work completed within the lot. In addition, all common areas and facilities within the scheme will be professionally cleaned and in a tidy condition and available for use by occupants of the scheme and, in particular, all debris, rubble, scrap and surplus building materials will be removed from the scheme and electricity and gas services will be available to the lot and the complex.

> B. This warranty is a fundamental term of this contract and has been inserted for the benefit of the Purchaser and may be waived by it by notice in writing to the Purchaser on or before settlement."

The single most common mistake investors make when buying units off the plan is agreeing to too short a settlement. Developers always require settlement in the minimum timeframe, which is generally 14 days from registration of title. Even in the most straightforward purchase of a unit off the plan, such a short timeframe places enormous pressures on solicitors and financiers for investors to settle on the due date. In Queensland, in particular, that date is "time of the essence". That is, if the investor doesn't settle on the 14th day then they're in default under the contract and the very least that can happen to them is that they'll lose their deposit. I think a minimum of 21 days is needed and ideally 30 days. It's amazing how easily developers will agree to 21 or even 30 days at the time of making the sale as they're keen to make the sale. The story is nearly always vastly different come settlement date when you request an extension for even a few days. The developer can impose substantial penalty interest if you're unable to settle on the agreed date.

32 HOW VALUABLE IS A RENTAL GUARANTEE?

In times of softening real estate markets, builders and developers become more sensitive to the anxieties of potential buyers of their new stock.

"How do we know that if we buy the new unit from you," the prospective buyer asks, "that we'll be able to rent the unit out for what you say?" "No problem," says the developer. "We have that covered. We're offering a rental guarantee for three years."

This was exactly the scenario presented to a new client of my firm recently. Upon production to us, as the buyer's solicitor, of the rental guarantee documentation we noted that it was offered not by the big-name developer itself but by an associated company of that developer. The moral of this story is that if you find yourself in a similar situation, as an investor, it's essential you make the contract subject to you satisfying yourself that the guarantee has been provided by a company with real assets and financial backing, hence the origin of this clause:

> "The Vendor acknowledges that the Purchaser is acquiring the unit on the basis that a company with substantial assets and financial standing guarantees the rental return from the unit for a period from completion. The Vendor also acknowledges that the Purchaser has no knowledge of the asset backing or financial standing of the company which has agreed to provide the rental guarantee.
>
> The Vendor must provide to the Purchaser within 14 days from the date of this contract details of the assets owned by that company and other information regarding its financial standing to allow the Purchaser to determine whether it is satisfied with the guarantee to be provided. If the Purchaser is not satisfied (in its sole discretion) regarding the asset backing and financial standing of the Guarantor company, and without being required to give any reason for doing so other than that it is not satisfied, the Purchaser may terminate this contract within 14 days of receipt of the information referred to above and in that event the deposit will be refunded to the Purchaser and this sale will be at an end."

Protecting your view

Perhaps it wasn't just the rental guarantee that lured you to buy that new unit but rather the fabulous views presented to you by the salesperson via the computer-generated images prepared by the developer. If you wouldn't have bought the unit apart from this inducement, then you must protect yourself by adding a clause along the following lines to the contract. When you read the clause you'll see that it's a balanced one from both parties' points of view as the developer has no control over what the owners of neighbouring properties do and how that affects your view.

"Representations on views

1. The Buyer acknowledges that the Seller has created photographs and computer-generated pictures as part of their marketing material which shows the potential view available from the units in the development from the practical completion of the building and the Seller acknowledges that these potential views have induced the Buyer to enter into this contract.

2. The Buyer acknowledges that the views are only potential views and the Seller gives no guarantees that the views from any particular unit will be as depicted in the marketing material because of development that may be carried out on an adjoining or nearby properties.

3. The Buyer acknowledges that the Seller has no control over development on properties surrounding or adjoining the lands or if any such developments may interfere with or interrupt the views from the unit that the Buyer has purchased as shown in the marketing material.

4. The Buyer will not make any claim for compensation or raise any objection or delay settlement if the views that

are available from the unit on practical completion of the building are not substantially the same views depicted in the marketing material because of any development carried out on adjoining or neighbouring lands after the date of this contract.

5. If, however, the views from the unit are not substantially the same as represented in the marketing material because of the construction of the building by the Seller the Buyer may terminate this contract, and in that event the deposit will be refunded to it and this matter will be at an end."

33 ARE THERE DIFFERENCES FOR OVERSEAS' INVESTORS BUYING OFF THE PLAN?

I took a phone call one week from an Australian client who had just returned from living in Scotland for 10 years. He was a good Aussie boy and had now returned to Australia with his new bride, who was a citizen of Great Britain but not Australia. They proposed to buy an upmarket unit off the plan and produced to me contract documentation to vet before they signed up.

I noticed in the contract an unusual clause that provided that if the buyer (they both proposed to purchase the unit) was registered for GST and could claim an input tax credit, then they must also pay GST to the seller on the sale. Another $200,000 would then be added to the purchase price. I discussed the matter with my newly returned Australian client and was surprised to find that he personally was registered for GST (he owned commercial property and GST was payable on the rental and therefore he had to lodge a Business Activity Statement return with the Australian Taxation Office). That fact then ruled him out as a purchaser and his next question was whether they could purchase the property in his wife's name (she wasn't registered for GST).

My advice to them was yes she could for the following reasons. It is lawful for foreigners to purchase a unit off the plan, provided the developer hasn't sold more than 50 per cent of the units in the complex off the plan to overseas' investors.

Developers can either obtain pre-approval to sell to foreigners in these circumstances (which the developer had done) or where this approval isn't obtained, an overseas' investor purchasing a property can apply themselves to the Foreign Investment Review Board (FIRB) for approval to purchase, which will be readily granted. The couple's next question to me was could they, he being an Australian citizen and she still being a citizen of Great Britain, purchase established residential real estate to live in as their home until their unit was built. My advice to them was that if his wife purchased an established property in her name only then she would need to apply for approval to purchase from the FIRB, which would be readily granted provided that she agreed to spend a minimum of 200 days per year in the property as her principal place of residence and didn't rent it out during the rest of the year. However, the good news was that if they purchased the property jointly then no approval at all was required for the purchase as the husband was an Australian citizen.

34 HOW CAN I INSURE AGAINST THE PROPERTY LOSING VALUE BEFORE I TAKE POSSESSION?

I call the answer to this dilemma, my 'silver bullet'.

So how do you protect yourself as the buyer of a new unit to be completed in a couple of years' time if there is a drop in the property's value between the date you contract to buy it and the date of settlement. Well, yes there is a clause that you can include in the contract of sale, if the seller will agree, whereby the price is adjusted, in a fair way I believe, to accommodate the drop in value.

Will the developer agree to such a clause? In a booming market they will not, of course, agree to such a clause but in a flat or falling market many of them will, and do. In a buyer's market then here is a clause that you can include in the contract. It makes interesting reading.

"a. The Seller acknowledges that the Buyer has purchased the property on the assumption that the property has a value not less than 95 per cent of the purchase price and the buyer's lender will be financing the purchase on that assumption.

b. The Seller also acknowledges that the Buyer's lender will be engaging a Valuer to undertake a valuation of the property on or about practical completion of the property and before settlement, and this contract is subject to the Valuer valuing the property for at least the purchase price, failing which the buyer may terminate this contract and in that event this matter will be at an end and the deposit refunded to the Buyer."

When you read this clause, it is clear that the matter may not proceed if the buyer's lender doesn't value the unit to at least 95 per cent of the purchase price.

If the buyer and the seller are prepared to proceed with the sale, if there's an adjustment downwards of the purchase price, an additional self-explanatory paragraph could be added to the above clause.

It is a fair solution between the interest of the buyer and the seller and is another example of how if you ask smart questions you can find an answer that will suit your situation.

Now that you are educated about this issue, add it to your catalogue of clauses that you have in your Investors Toolbox. More power to you as an investor.

> "c. Without limiting the buyer's right to terminate this Contract of Sale under paragraph (b), the buyer may elect to settle the purchase of the property, and if it does so, the purchase price payable on settlement will be reduced and calculated as follows:
>
> Purchase Price will be the Contract price less 50 per cent of the difference between the Purchase Price stated in this contract and the valuation referred to in paragraph (a) above."
>
> (Example: the property is valued at $360,000 and the contract price is $400,000. The reduced purchase price is: $400,000 less $360,000 = $40,000.00 divided by 50 per cent = $20,000. Reduced purchase price = $400,000 less $20,000 = $380,000.)

Finally, what if the property was valued at 50 per cent less than the purchase price and the developer just didn't want to be forced to sell at such a decreased price?

It is reasonable in these circumstances to add the following extra paragraph to the clause which allows the seller to terminate the sale:

> "d. If the Buyer elects to proceed and settle the purchase of the property at the purchase price calculated as set out in paragraph (c) then the Contract is further subject to the Seller being satisfied with the amount of the reduced purchase price, failing which the Seller may terminate this Contract of Sale and in that event this matter will be at an end and the deposit refunded to the Buyer."

Before Christmas I was sharing a glass of red with a Queensland developer John Potter who at the bottom of the GFC was still standing (yes, I know – almost an endangered species).

Our conversation moved to the discussion of this silver bullet.

He agreed that this clause was a fair solution to the buyer's dilemma when the value of the property dropped between the contract date and completion of the building and settlement which is often a year or two later.

John Potter went on to say, "It's a bit of a 'claw back' for the buyer. I would be prepared to agree to such a clause in my sale contracts as long as it worked both ways. So if the property went up in value then there would be a 'claw forward' (e.g. the purchase price would go up 50 per cent of the difference between the contract price and the valuation figure)."

So here is one last clause on the subject:

> "e. If the Valuer referred to in paragraph (a) values the property at more than the contract price then the

purchase price paid by the buyer on settlement will be increased and calculated as follows:

Purchase price will be the contract price plus 50 per cent of the difference between the purchase price stated in this contract and the valuation referred to in paragraph (a) above."

If the buyer, even if presented with a strong valuation, still didn't wish to proceed with the purchase (e.g. the higher purchase price meant that their borrowings were way beyond their comfort zone, or their lender wouldn't lend them the extra money because of their income level), the next extra self-explanatory paragraph set out below could be added at the end of the clause:

"If paragraph (e) above applies, this contract is further subject to the Buyer being satisfied with the amount of the increased purchase price, failing which the Buyer may terminate this contract, and in that event this matter will be at an end and the deposit will be refunded to the buyer."

What are the benefits of buying off the plan?

It's important to keep some balance between the pros and the cons when looking at buying units off the plan. It's not all negative as some readers might believe and as might appear from my questions regarding the downsides of this strategy. To put some balance in the ledger between the positives and the negatives, it shouldn't be forgotten that buying units off the plan has the following benefits:

1. The long settlement allows for the real potential for capital growth.

2. The cost of providing the deposit is a lot lower as a bank deposit can be provided rather than the cash

amount (bank deposits can be provided for a cost of around 2 per cent per annum).

3. There is the opportunity to on-sell the property to help your cash flow in the year that you settle the purchase.

4. If the settlement date is more than a year off, the property can be re-valued close to settlement and if there has been capital gain it may be possible to finance 100 per cent of the purchase price.

35 IF I AM SECOND OR THIRD BUYER OFF THE PLAN – WHAT ARE THE PITFALLS?

When the market gathers momentum, clients buy more units off the plan, but not from the developer – instead, from the initial purchaser.

As a market picks up speed, you can expect to see more on-sales from the second and third purchasers. The first thing to realise when buying off the plan and on-selling is that there's no way to avoid payment of stamp duty. The Office of State Revenue collects stamp duty on each of the purchases, which is one of the reasons for the massive spike in stamp duty revenue received by state governments during real estate booms.

The second thing to realise is that these sales and on-sales rely upon the "domino effect" to achieve settlement and if one of the buyers along the way falters or trips, then the whole scenario collapses like a pack of cards (or dominos). You must realise, then, that as one of the buyers who is on-selling, you're not off the hook until the last of the sales settles. That is, if the person buying from you fails to settle, you're still liable to settle the purchase. As you'll usually be relying on the subsequent purchaser's money to fund the transaction, no plans will usually be in place to provide for this contingency and you'll then be in default of your obligation under the contract of sale (resulting, at least, in a loss of your deposit and an exposure to a claim by the developer for any further loss it suffers). This can mean a lot of sleepless nights until the settlement actually takes place. This is one of the reasons that purchasing and on-selling units off the plan is a risky business.

Here's another twist. A client told me they were buying a unit off the plan, but their seller was the first buyer, making my client the second buyer of the unit off the plan. They advised me they were borrowing 90 per cent of the purchase price. I explained to them that the developer wouldn't be transferring the title to the unit to them as the second purchaser, but instead they'd receive a prior stamped transfer from the developer to their seller (as the first purchaser) and then a signed transfer from their seller to themselves on settlement, upon which they would have to pay stamp duty. I alerted them to the fact that their lender might feel anxious about this because of the possibility that someone could interpose a dealing with the property in between the two transfers, for example a mortgage or a caveat.

Sure enough, this was precisely their lender's concern. This anxiety was heightened by the fact that the client's equity in the property was only 10 per cent. The lender advised that it required an injection of 20 per cent equity or the provision of additional real estate security for the loan. The client could provide neither.

How could this play of events have been avoided?

The inclusion of a clause in the contract of sale, that the first purchaser (as seller to my client) arrange for the developer to sign a transfer by direction to my client as second buyer, would have solved the problem. The transfer of title would go straight from the developer to the second purchaser, thus relieving the anxiety of the lender.

This solution sounds simple, but it isn't.

The reason being that the developer has no obligation to provide a transfer by direction. But why shouldn't they, you ask? A mercenary developer might be happy to let the second sale fall in a heap because of this problem resulting in the consequent collapse of its first sale (because that buyer is relying on the money from the on-sale to fund the purchase).

The developer would then retain the first buyer's deposit, terminate the first contract and eventually on-sell the unit for, say, another $50,000 itself.

What a cruel world, you might despair. Yes it is, and you'll be eaten alive unless you educate yourself more about these issues before buying and selling off the plan.

> *"Shaw: I have reserved two tickets for you for my premiere. Come and bring a friend – if you have one.*
>
> *Churchill: Sorry I can't be there for the first performance. Will attend the second – if there is one."*
>
> GEORGE BERNARD SHAW AND
> WINSTON CHURCHILL

Part VI
SMART QUESTIONS CONCERNING DEPOSITS

An optimist sees an opportunity in every calamity; a pessimist sees calamity in every opportunity.

ANONYMOUS

Smart Questions Concerning Deposits

When it comes to special conditions in contracts and issues relating to contracts of sale, there is no more humble an issue than the deposit. I mean, what is there to know? So why does this topic warrant a whole part in this book? Well, you have come this far so read on and understand that building your knowledge about even an apparently simple matter such as the deposit will make you grow strong as an investor.

> *"Journalist: Who wears the pants in your house?*
> *Thatcher: I do. I also wash and iron them."*
>
> DENNIS THATCHER, HUSBAND OF MARGARET

36 DO I NEED TO PAY A DEPOSIT?

Legally, the answer is no. A deposit isn't needed to have a binding and enforceable contract for the sale of a property. For those of you who have studied the law of contracts you may well ask what the 'consideration' is (the consideration being one of the six elements required to constitute a binding contract).

The answer is – the deposit is not the consideration. It's the "stake" paid by you, as security that you will honour your agreement to buy the property in 30 days' time. The "consideration" is the amount of money that you'll pay to the seller on settlement date in 30 days' time. The parties can agree to have no stake or deposit, and still have a binding contract.

37 HOW MUCH SHOULD THE DEPOSIT BE?

It helps in answering this question to put yourself in the sellers' shoes. From their viewpoint the deposit is "hurt money". That is, what you will lose as a buyer if you don't complete the purchase after signing up to do so. Ideally, a seller would ask for a deposit of 10 per cent of the purchase price, or at least 5 per cent of the purchase price.

Five per cent of the purchase price is still a satisfactory amount to pay as a deposit. After all, 5 per cent of the sale price at $300,000 is $15,000. As buyers, very few people will walk away from a $15,000 deposit simply because they've had a change of heart about the property. From the perspective of a buyer, the deposit should be as little as possible, for obvious reasons.

The issue is usually resolved in the marketplace by the real estate agent who will be extremely reluctant to promote any offer where the deposit doesn't at least cover the amount of their commission. This is more evidence of a theme that I've been promoting recently that the most powerful person in the transaction isn't the buyer or the seller, but is nearly always the real estate agent.

Whatever the amount the deposit ultimately is, remember to initially only put down a token deposit of say $1,000, with the balance to be payable within two to three working days after you sign off on all of your special conditions (finance, building inspection, etc.). If the purchase doesn't proceed because finance isn't approved or there are pest and building problems, the less of your cash that the agent holds, the better. There's no incentive for the seller or agent to argue about refunding a deposit of $1,000 but there could be if a deposit of say $40,000 is paid.

Our office was recently involved in a case where we acted for a buyer who signed up to buy a property for $300,000 and paid a deposit of $30,000. The contract was subject to finance and a pest and building inspection. The client was unhappy with the outcome of the pest and building inspection. Although the report showed there was only minor pest infestation, there was clear evidence of regular but expensive treatment of the property over the years to contain the pest problem. Although the problem was minor now, it would only stay that way if the buyer maintained an expensive maintenance and treatment program on the house. The seller objected strongly to the buyer's termination on these grounds and said that the pest problem was minor only. The seller did not accept the buyer was entitled to terminate the contract because of the heavy ongoing maintenance costs of controlling the pest issue. He argued that the buyer had not acted in good faith and refused to release the deposit. The matter was eventually resolved.

The buyer did not wish to pursue legal action and sacrificed $10,000 of the deposit monies. He authorised the agent to release that amount to the seller in return for the release of the majority of the deposit. This was a $10,000 mistake made by an uneducated investor who did not speak to us before he signed the contract. If only a token deposit of $1,000 had been paid with the balance of $29,000 payable within two working days of satisfaction of the pest and building report, the seller would have had no financial incentive to apply pressure in this way. He simply would have authorised the release of the deposit without any argument.

The moral of the story then is to only pay a token deposit e.g. $1,000 with the balance payable later.

Allow a proper period of time to pay the balance of the deposit

Ensure that you allow yourself a proper period of time to pay the balance of the deposit once you go unconditional, e.g. at least two working days from satisfaction of all special conditions. In particular, don't agree to pay the balance deposit on "approval of finance" or "satisfaction of pest and building reports". Such wording will require you to pay the balance deposit that day, or certainly no later than the next day. If you pay it two or three days later then you will be in breach of the contract entitling the seller to retain the whole of the deposit (including the balance that you have just now paid) because of your breach.

A suitable clause for payment of a split deposit would be as follows:

> "The deposit will be paid to the Deposit Holder as follows:
>
> $1,000 within two (2) working days of formation of this Contract; and
>
> Balance deposit of (completed amount) within two (2) working days of satisfaction or waiver of the last of the special conditions."

38 DOES THE DEPOSIT HAVE TO BE IN CASH?

Where large amounts of money are to be paid as a deposit and held by an agent pending a long settlement, say $50,000 or more over a six-month period, you should be aware of a product called a "power bond" or a "deposit bond" (sometimes called a deposit guarantee).

Sellers regularly agree to accept these in place of a deposit. The way they work is that they are an unconditional guarantee by a lender that if you default under your contract as a buyer, they will pay the amount of the deposit at that time. They are usually lodged with the real estate agent at the same time the deposit would have been paid, and are returned to the lender following settlement. They usually last for up to a year (they have to be renewed if there's a settlement date further away than a year). They cost 1 to 2 per cent of the amount covered by the guarantee and a special clause has to be added to the contract to deal with this issue.

39 SHOULD I RELEASE THE DEPOSIT BEFORE SETTLEMENT?

It's not advisable to release the deposit to the seller before settlement, as these monies may never be recovered if completion doesn't take place. For example, the seller may go bankrupt or some other person may lodge a caveat (a freeze on the title) before settlement and therefore prohibit settlement from proceeding. The risk you take when you release the deposit can be minimised by adding a clause to the contract which makes the contract subject to your solicitor receiving the results of your searches of the property and these being to the solicitor's satisfaction, before monies are released. A sample clause is set out below:

> "The Buyer authorises the stakeholder to release the deposit to the Seller once the Buyer's solicitors have received the results of all of their searches of the property and provided that they are satisfied with the results of those searches.
>
> The Buyer's solicitors must advise the Seller's solicitor in writing within (complete) days from the date of this

Contract whether they have received and are satisfied or not about the results of their searches."

You may still be anxious about releasing the deposit, even after you've conducted your searches of the property, as you may be fearful that the property may be mortgaged to 95 per cent of its value and once 10 per cent is released to the seller the balance of 90 per cent is insufficient to pay out the seller's mortgage on settlement. You can protect yourself against this possibility by adding a clause to the contract that obliges the seller to produce a letter from their lender saying that it will release the mortgage on settlement, upon payment of the balance of the purchase price (and release of the deposit to the seller) and this letter has to be produced to you before settlement. A sample clause is set out below:

> "The Seller warrants that the property is subject to one mortgage only to (complete) (The 'Mortgagee'). The Seller agrees to produce to the Buyer's solicitors evidence in writing acceptable to the Buyer's solicitors from the Mortgagee that upon payment of the balance purchase price on completion, the Mortgagee will release its mortgage over the property and pass unencumbered title to the property to the Buyer.
>
> This Contract is subject to the Seller producing that evidence to the Buyer's solicitors within 14 days from the date of this Contract, failing which the deposit will be refunded to the Buyer and this sale will be at an end apart from any rights either of the parties may have against the other as a result of any breach of this Contract."

If the seller tells you the property isn't mortgaged at all then this can obviously be verified when your solicitor undertakes their search of the property, or the following clause can be added to the contract:

"The Seller warrants that the property is not subject to any mortgage. The Seller's warranty contained in this special condition is a fundamental term of this Contract which has been added for the benefit of the Buyer and may be waivered by him/her at any time in writing before settlement."

40 SHOULD I AGREE TO RELEASE OF THE DEPOSIT TO ALLOW THE SELLER TO BUY ANOTHER PROPERTY?

The standard conditions of contracts in common use in Australia provide that the deposit is to be released to the seller on settlement of the sale. This provision is for the buyer's protection to ensure that no monies are payable to the seller until title passes to the buyer. But what if you're the seller and the property you've sold is your home? You now want to buy a new home but don't have enough money to put down as a deposit. Can a deposit paid by your buyer be released to you so that it can be placed as a deposit on another property being acquired by you with the settlement to take place simultaneously with your sale?

In these circumstances the risk of the loss of the deposit following its release lessens because of the purpose for which the monies are to be released. The risk is reduced because the money will still be held in the real estate agent's trust account as the stakeholder on the purchase of another property, particularly if the same agent is making both sales.

An appropriate clause to include in the first contract is set out below:

> "If requested by the Seller, the Deposit Holder must release $(insert amount to be released) from the deposit for the benefit of the seller.
>
> However, the sum to be released must be paid by the Deposit Holder to a real estate agent to be held as a deposit on the purchase of real estate by the Seller.
>
> The Seller will only be entitled to make a request under this clause if clause 3 (finance) and 4 (building inspection) of the Terms of Contract are not applicable, or have either been satisfied or waived."

At the end of the day, releasing deposits is always a risky strategy and is best avoided if at all possible. My comments in this section are only "belts and braces" attempting to minimise the risk, not remove it.

"Q. What do you wear in bed?
Marilyn Monroe: Chanel No 5."

Part VII
SMART QUESTIONS ABOUT OPTIONS, RIGHTS OF FIRST REFUSAL AND PRELIMINARY AGREEMENTS

I used to be Snow White, but I drifted.

MAE WEST

Smart Questions About Options, Rights of First Refusal and Preliminary Agreements

You will be realising by now, that the answer to many of the smart questions is to include an additional clause in the contract of sale, to put your mind at rest.

Many real estate agents and investors operate under the principle that "Less is Yes", that is, the less clauses you have in a contract of sale the more chance you have of getting a "Yes" from the seller. There is a lot of truth to that statement but don't let that be the sole driving force behind what you do. I am a firm believer that creative use of clauses can lead to a deal where previously, working under the cloud of ignorance, there was not a deal to be had.

This is why my mandate is educate yourself as an investor to learn how to use clauses creatively about such things as vendor finance, instalment contracts, trades, back-up contract clauses and sunset clauses. Educate yourself now about how to put property on lay-by until you make up your mind whether to buy it (through the use of options). Understand, too, the difference between an option and a right of first refusal and when it is best not to use a contract of sale at all, but instead proceed by way of a preliminary agreement (sometimes called a letter of intent or heads of agreement).

So let's continue on our path of self-education with the topics of options, rights of first refusal and preliminary agreements.

> *"When I meet a new man I ask myself, 'Is this the man I want my children to spend their weekend access visits with?'"*
>
> RITA RUDNER, AMERICAN COMEDIAN

41 WHAT IS THE DIFFERENCE BETWEEN AN OPTION AND A RIGHT OF FIRST REFUSAL?

A property investor advised me that he and the owner of the property had agreed that he would have first option to buy this property in the next six months and asked me if I could do something simple to document this agreement. I asked him:

1. What was the purchase price for the property, should the first option be exercised?
2. When would settlement take place?
3. What was the amount of the deposit?

I also asked some other questions about details that are normally included in a formal contract of sale.

It was clear to me that he hadn't agreed to take an option to buy the property, but had simply been given a right of first refusal. There's a fundamental difference between these two concepts.

An option to purchase gives the buyer of the property the right, but not the obligation, to buy the property within, say, a six-month period. It allows the investor to put the property on lay-by and during the next six months make up their mind about whether they wish to purchase the property or not. It's essential, however, that the exact terms of the contract that comes into existence if the option is exercised are finalised at the time the option is granted, for example purchase price, settlement date, deposit, etc.

A right of first refusal has been described by the High

Court of Australia as "worthless". It means that if the owner of the property at some time in the future decides to sell the property – and they don't have to – they agree to first advise you that it's now available for purchase. That purchase will be on whatever terms and price they determine and, once they've made you aware that it's for sale, then they've discharged their obligations to you. It's for this reason the High Court says it's worthless.

From a more practical point of view, and not the lofty heights of the highest court in the land, a right of first refusal does have some value. It's worth something to be the first person to know that a property is for sale, as you can then at least take the initiative and attempt to buy it.

The basics of a right of first refusal

An elderly client had just sold his old fibro cottage to a developer to be used as part of a site for a new unit development. He really liked the area and asked what clause he could add to his contract of sale so that he could have the first chance to buy a unit on the ground floor of the new unit building if he liked the look of it. The developer hadn't even prepared concept plans at this stage for his building, so it wasn't possible to prepare a binding and enforceable option in favour of my client. Such an option would give my client the right to take the initiative on completion of the building and insist the developer sell the unit to him. Not enough information was available at this stage to prepare such a document. My client simply wanted to have the first chance to buy the property if he liked the quality of it once completed.

A simple clause set out below was then added to the contract:

"A. The Purchaser agrees, should it construct a unit development on the lands following Settlement, to offer the Vendor the first right to purchase any one unit in the complex selected by the Purchaser on whatever terms and conditions the Vendor is offering such units for sale.

B. In the event that the Vendor does not enter into a binding and enforceable Contract with the Purchaser in relation to the sale of such unit within 14 days of being offered such unit for sale, then the Vendor's rights under this clause will extinguish and thereafter the Vendor will have no further rights against the purchaser in relation to this matter."

42 WILL REAL ESTATE AGENTS HELP YOU FIND OPTION PROPERTIES?

In almost every case not only won't they help you, they won't even understand the concept. Understand also that agents' commission is based on the sale price of a property.

Therefore, there is little incentive for a real estate agent to source for you a property and assist you in negotiating a call option with the prospect of an on-sale of the call option for say $50,000 to $100,000. You will understand why they would prefer you to buy the property for $500,000 (they receive a commission on that figure), settle the purchase, obtain the approvals which add the extra value and then on-sell the property again for $550,000 to $600,000 and they receive commission on that sale price as well. It doesn't take you long to realise then that with the options strategy you will almost always be on your own in sourcing the property and of course 'on-selling it'.

43 WHY WOULD A SELLER SIGN A CALL OPTION AGREEMENT?

In some instances, sellers are lured by the amount of the option fee where it is in the order of $5,000 to $10,000 cash or more. They often see this as 'quick cash' and are attracted by it.

They may also have had real troubles, up until your approach, in selling the property at all and feel they have nothing to lose in giving you the right for a short period of time to buy the property, i.e. let you put it on lay-by.

Alternatively, they may have had some offers to buy the property but you are the first person who is prepared to meet their price. Perhaps because you can see the value in the property if you obtain an approval to develop it or use it for a higher usage.

So, as you can see, options aren't for beginners. But they are worth having in your arsenal as an investor to be drawn out when an opportunity arises.

44 WHERE DO YOU FIND PROPERTIES OVER WHICH THE SELLERS MIGHT GRANT YOU A CALL OPTION?

If you are looking to trade a unit for a boat or another piece of real estate then you can place an ad in, or visit, the exchange/trade sections of the real estate pages of your local newspaper.

If you are looking for a partner to undertake a joint venture, you could perhaps ask around your circle of friends or fellow investors for people with like-minds who might entertain the idea.

Alternatively, you might type 'real estate joint ventures' into a Google search and see where it leads you. It is not as simple as this with options. It will be up to you to source the vendors yourself. You will need to find a vendor who is attracted to the idea of entering into a call option because, for example, they have had trouble selling their property or problems securing the price they were after. You (unlike others before you) might see the value in the property at the price they are asking, but only if you can do something yourself to add value, such as obtain development approval. Therefore, acreage land (future development sites) are commonly the subject of call option agreements. Houses suitable for renovation are not, as there is simply not enough in it to justify the effort, time and money required to secure a call option. You might as well just buy the property, renovate it and then on-sell it after you have completed the renovation.

45 PRELIMINARY AGREEMENTS – PAPERWORK WORTH DOING?

Thousands of dollars in lawyers' time and countless hours of investors' time are burnt every day in the property world in failed attempts to negotiate real estate contracts.

"Is there a less frustrating, more time- and cost-efficient way to go about negotiating real estate deals?" one jaded client asked me recently. "There sure is," I replied, "use a form of preliminary agreement to reach initial agreement on the basic terms of the transaction and once you've done that you can then move forward comfortably to settle the wording of the formal agreements."

Many of the more complicated commercial and industrial transactions, joint ventures and property syndications are brought together this way and avoid wasting time and legal costs in deals that don't proceed. These preliminary agreements are given a variety of badges, however the main ones are:

1. Heads of agreement
2. Offer and acceptance
3. Letter of intent
4. Memorandum of understanding (MOU).

Motives and strategies for using them

Apart from the cost and time-savings, there are many and varied other reasons to use these legal documents:

1. To have something more concrete to show other prospective joint venturers and syndicate members;
2. To provide a level of commitment to the transaction to the other party;
3. To have something fundamental to show financiers to gauge their level of interest in the transaction;
4. For the ever-increasing number of companies that require approval from directors before expending the company's resources, to obtain board approval to proceed in a substantial way.

There are downsides, though, to using preliminary agreements. They add an extra layer to the documentation for the transaction, often resulting in delays in concluding final contracts and sometimes loss of the deal. So investors should always ask themselves, is a preliminary agreement really necessary or should they just "jump in" with formal contracts.

Finessing the deal

One of my developer clients called me about preliminary agreements and said that there is always a threshold issue with these agreements, which is: "How binding are they?". I recommend to investors that they put the matter beyond any doubt by adding one of two conditions to the preliminary agreement: one which states that the agreement did constitute a legally binding and enforceable agreement; or the other, the reverse, that is – execution of the preliminary agreement didn't create a legally binding and enforceable contract and only created a statement of their intention.

My client's take on the matter was from his angle as a developer. As a developer he was always trying to tie up development sites without frightening sellers away or worse still, prompting them by the terms of the preliminary agreement to take the document off to their solicitor. He said to me, "Rob, you know how many deals are lost once the paperwork is taken to a solicitor," which is a fair comment.

His perspective on these agreements was to draft them so that there's a strong possibility that they're legally binding without actually using the words "legally binding and enforceable agreement", which would prompt sellers to race off and see their solicitor or scare them off. He, therefore, always inserts at the end of preliminary agreements that he presents to owners of property the following clause:

> "The remaining terms of the agreement between the parties will be on the standard terms and conditions utilised by the Real Estate Institute and/or the Law Society for contracts of a similar nature, but excluding any other special terms, and otherwise on reasonable terms and conditions."

Investors who now wish to finesse the deal by adding a similar clause to their preliminary agreements should, of course, first consult their own legal adviser and obtain specific advice on their circumstances before attempting this strategy. Sellers should be aware the developers are almost always more street-smart than they are and therefore should always show the agreement to their solicitor before signing.

"When they told me that by the year 2000 women would rule the world, my reply was 'Still?'"

WINSTON CHURCHILL,
FORMER BRITISH PRIME MINISTER

Part VIII

SMART QUESTIONS ABOUT SEARCHES, INVESTIGATIONS AND DUE DILIGENCE

At a casino, Kerry Packer asked why someone was getting a lot of attention from staff. He was told that he was a wealthy Texan oilman worth $100 million.

Kerry Packer: Really? $100 million?

Oilman: Yes, I am sir.

Kerry Packer: I'll toss you for it, son.

Smart Questions About Searches, Investigations and Due Diligence

By now my catchcry of education and more education should be starting to sink in, even for the slow learners amongst you. It is only through education that you can take the right action to avoid the slippery slopes of property investment.

It does require some energy though. As tempting as it is to leave these issues to others and to flick the problems to your solicitors and accountants, I would encourage you not to do so. The reason is that the easy road eventually becomes the hard road. My message to you then is to put the effort now into your own instruction and the hard road will eventually become easy.

So, continuing on with my instructions for you on how to become a better generalist, let me take you through some frequently asked questions about searches and investigations an investor might make on a property purchase and the issue of due diligence.

This part of the book contains some of the smarter questions investors ask about these issues.

> *"If you think education is expensive, try the cost of ignorance."*
>
> WARREN BUFFETT

46 WHAT IS A DUE DILIGENCE?

The property you are buying may require a more exhaustive investigation of quite a number of matters. A general due diligence clause that makes the contract subject to you carrying out investigations and enquiries, and being satisfied with the results of these enquiries, would be appropriate.

"A. This agreement is conditional upon the buyer conducting investigations and enquiries ('the enquiries') about the property and all related matters and being satisfied with the results of the enquiries including and without limitation:
   (a) a survey of the property;
   (b) a building inspection and engineer's report of any structures on the property;
   (c) the terms of any Grants of Easement registered on the title to the property;
   (d) any lease and/or licence agreements relating to any use of the property;
   (e) zoning and the lawful use of the property;
   (f) the requirements of any local or other competent authority having jurisdiction over the property and the terms of any permits, approvals, consents and requisitions of any local or other government authorities;
   (g) fire safety matters;
   (h) termite and pest inspections of all improvements on the property;
   (i) any encroachments by or on the adjoining properties;
   (j) soil tests;
   (k) workplace health and safety matters;

(l) any other matter deemed by the buyer to be relevant to the purchase.

B. The buyer will meet any expense of carrying out the enquiries and the buyer will do so entirely at its own risk and will indemnify the seller against all claims or demands that may be made against the seller or which the seller may suffer because of the buyer carrying out the enquiries. The buyer will also reinstate any damage that it may cause to the property during the course of carrying out the enquiries.

C. The seller will permit the buyer and its representatives access to the property at all reasonable times to carry out the enquiries.

D. The buyer will be allowed a period of twenty-one (21) days from the date of this contract in which to conduct the enquiries.

E. If the buyer is not satisfied with the results of the enquiries then the buyer may, in its absolute discretion and without being required to give any reasons, deliver written notice to the seller terminating this contract at any time on or before 5pm on the date being twenty-three (23) days from the date of this contract.

In that event this agreement will be at an end, the deposit must be refunded to the buyer and after that neither party will have any further claim or action against the other apart from a claim based on a default by one party under the contract prior to termination.

F. This clause has been inserted for the benefit of the buyer and the buyer may at any time by notice in writing to the seller waive the benefit of this clause."

Don't become a casualty with your due diligence

I received a call from a client who'd entered into a contract to buy a property in a residential zone that allowed a three-storey townhouse development. It was a corner block which gave it extra exposure, theoretically greater value and therefore good prospects of selling the townhouses.

The contract was subject to undertaking due diligence and a feasibility study of building a small unit development on the site. The seller and the agent both said a successful small unit development could be constructed on the site. My client wanted to leave no stone unturned and engaged me to do a full round of enquiries and investigations such as a survey, town planning report, title and main road check and a costing on creating a body corporate structure containing townhouses.

The matter fell flat on its face and he terminated the contract of sale when he found out that the property's dual road frontage was a double-edged sword. While it gave great exposure to the property and greater accessibility, council town planning officers advised that the building had to be set back from both the road frontages. The block was smaller than the average residential block and once 6 metre setbacks were applied to each of the two road frontages there was little land left on which to construct any worthwhile unit development.

At the end of the day my client's best advice from his consultants was that the property was really only suited to one dwelling and any units that could be built on the site would be so small as to be unmarketable.

My client added up the thrown away costs of engaging lawyers, town planners, etc. which ran into the thousands of dollars. His question for me was, did he have recourse against the seller or the agent because their representations were incorrect. My advice to him was that as there was no guarantee in the contract promising the correctness of the representations, it was a case of "buyer beware".

The moral of this story is to make as many verbal enquiries as you can about these matters before you commit to the contract and potentially throw away lots of money on due diligence. A few telephone enquiries to the town planning officers at the local authority to verify the sales talk from the seller and their agent could save you time and money.

47 CAN I APPLY FOR BUILDING AND DEVELOPMENT APPROVAL OVER A PROPERTY THAT I DON'T YET OWN?

With some property purchases, you may need to make an application to the council regarding your plans for it. For example, you might need building approval or approval to re-site a house on a property so that you can subdivide it and create an additional block of land. You will need to obtain the seller's consent to make such applications, and therefore the following clause should be inserted in the contract:

> "In the event that the Buyer wishes to make application for approval by the local authority or any other government department or statutory authority for development of the property (including building approval), the Seller agrees to join in and consent to such application and sign all documents and do everything that is reasonably necessary for the purposes of the Buyer's application, provided the Buyer pays all costs and expenses associated with the application."

This clause allows you to make an application before you are the owner. Without such a clause you have no such right.

What about the right to conduct legal due diligence – but with the contract not subject to it?

A couple of my clients contacted me to advise that they had secured the purchase of a property which they would develop. Settlement was six months away. I was told that it was essential to the seller that they had an unconditional contract. However, it was just as important to my clients that they had the right before settlement to undertake all of their investigations and enquiries about the site and not have to wait until settlement (six months later) to do so. The clients asked me to draft a clause which gave them the right to carry out investigations but the contract was not subject to the results of those investigations. Set out below is such a clause. Without such a clause in the contract, the buyer had no right to carry out these investigations and could have lost six months of valuable time.

"A. The Vendor acknowledges that the Purchaser is undertaking investigations and enquiries about the property and various related matters, although this Contract is not subject to the outcome of such investigations and enquiries.

B. The Purchaser will meet any expense of carrying out the enquiries and will do so entirely at its own risk. It will also indemnify the Vendor against all claims or demands that may be made against the Vendor or which the Vendor may suffer because of the Purchaser carrying out these investigations and enquiries. The Purchaser will reinstate the property because of any damage that it may cause to the property during the course of carrying out the investigations and enquiries.

C. The Vendor will permit the Purchaser and its representatives access to the property at all reasonable times."

48. PEST AND BUILDING INSPECTIONS – WHAT ARE THE TRAPS WITH THE STANDARD CLAUSES IN CONTRACTS USED BY AGENTS?

Real estate agents regularly insert a special condition to the contract watering down a buyer's normal rights in respect to pest and building inspections. The special conditions added by the agent usually provide that in order for the buyer to be able to terminate the contract because of a pest or building problem the building problem must be one that creates 'structural unsoundness' or the pest problem must be a 'manifest pest infestation'.

What in the world does all this mean?

You should simply strike out these offensive clauses before signing and add either or both of the following clauses which clearly give you the right to pull out because you are not happy with any aspect of the building inspection or pest inspection.

"(a) Subject to building inspection

The Seller acknowledges that the Buyers wish to arrange for an inspection of all improvements on the land by a builder of their choice. After reasonable notice, the Sellers must allow a builder of the Buyers' choice access to the land and inside the improvements on the land for the purposes of carrying out an inspection of the improvements.

This Contract is subject to the Buyers and the builder selected by the Buyers being satisfied with the results of the inspection of the improvements within (complete) days from the date of this Contract, failing which this Contract will be at an end, the deposit refunded to the Buyer and neither party will have any claim against the other apart from any rights either of the parties may have against the other as a result of any breach of this Contract.

(b) Subject to pest inspection

The Sellers acknowledge that the Buyers wish to undertake an inspection of the lands and all improvements on the lands to ascertain whether there are any problems with pests or termites.

After reasonable notice the Sellers must allow a pest/termite exterminator or investigator of the Buyers' choice access to the lands and inside any improvements on the lands for the purpose of carrying out an inspection.

This contract is subject to the Buyers being satisfied with the results of the inspection within (complete) days from the date of this contract, failing which this contract will be at an end, the deposit refunded to the Buyer and neither party will have any claim against the other apart from any rights either of the parties may have against the other as a result of any breach of this Contract."

I can't stress enough how important it is when you buy a house to engage a qualified, experienced builder to undertake a building inspection. I recommend to all my clients that they engage someone who is independent of the real estate agent who sold them the property. If you don't know of such a builder, you can contact the Housing Industry Association or Master Builders Association and ask them to recommend the services of one of their members.

The right person should prepare for you a separately typed

report for your property and should have no problem meeting you onsite to allow you to watch them carrying out the inspection.

Beware 'tick box' building inspectors whose report comprises a one-page typed sheet with a tick or cross in the appropriate boxes.

One of my clients came to grief not that long ago when they accepted the agent's recommendation to use a 'tick box' building inspector who failed to locate a structural problem in the roof which cost $15,000 to repair.

The builder didn't even take the lazy man's way out, climb onto a ladder and shine his torch into the roof where the problem would instantly have revealed itself to him.

When challenged about his oversight his only comment was that he undertook a fixed-price service to look at the items mentioned on his one-page sheet (the roof wasn't included) and if additional work was required (e.g. checking the roof), it should have been requested and an additional fee would have been payable. What a costly mistake.

49 THERMAL IMAGING – WHAT WILL IT PICK UP THAT MY BUILDER MIGHT MISS?

A novice investor called me to sign off on a pest and building report. He was delighted with the outcome of the report and was pleased to tell me that the inspectors backed up the physical check with a thermal imaging scan of the property.

This meant that for an extra $120 the inspector carried out a thermal scan (X-ray) of the property. The scan showed up areas that may have been water-damaged but covered over cosmetically by new carpet or a coat of paint. These areas will still have residual dampness which will show up as blue in colour on a scan but will be undetectable to the naked eye. Similarly, termite areas show up on these extremely sensitive scans as red because of the energy generated from the activity from the termites.

"How good is that?" was his comment to me. "Why would you spend hundreds of thousands of dollars on a property and not pay the extra $120 for this scan?" I agree.

50 ZONING – HOW IMPORTANT IS IT?

The importance of zoning can never be underestimated, particularly when you're purchasing a commercial property. A long-time client consulted me recently seeking advice about buying a property on an arterial road leading into one of Australia's capital cities. The property has been used as a caryard and was subject to a lease for 10 years to a car dealer at a rental of close to $100,000 per annum.

This gave the property a commercial value of around a million dollars. When I suggested to my client that we make the contract subject to checking that the zoning of the property allowed it to be used as a caryard (the lease contained a guarantee from the owner and all subsequent owners that it was lawful to use the property as a caryard, failing which the lease came to an end), my client told me I worried too much about such things and reminded me that the property had been used for more than 30 years to sell cars. In the end, he reluctantly agreed to make the offer subject to us carrying out a search of the zoning of the property, which the seller accepted.

My client was startled to find out the property had never been approved for use as a caryard and if this fact ever came to the attention of the tenant or the council then this would probably bring about an end to the use and the lease. Our enquiries revealed that its use as a caryard maximised the return from the property and a rental of only $50,000 a year could be obtained for any other commercial use.

As commercial properties are sold on yield, if the property eventually had to be leased for some other use it would only have the value of half a million dollars and not the $1 million our client agreed to pay for it. The matter didn't proceed and now my client doesn't tell me I worry too much. Instead he jokes, "Rob Balanda for Mayor".

51 WHEN DO I NEED TO MAKE MY CONTRACT SUBJECT TO AN ENVIRONMENTAL CHECK?

Calls from three different clients in one week buying land on which they wanted to construct new homes brought home to me the importance of considering environmental issues. Let's look at it further.

If you purchase a property which was once, say, part of a farm, the block you're purchasing may have once been part of a cattle dip. Alternatively, the land may have been the site of a service station. It may be necessary to excavate all of the land which was once a cattle dip, or where the petrol tanks were situated in the case of a service station, refill that land with clean soil and then compact it so that it will hold a new building. This can be extremely expensive and it's essential therefore to make the contract subject to checks with the appropriate environmental agency and consultants to ensure this isn't an issue.

A sample clause is:

> "This Contract is subject to the Buyer undertaking any enquiries and investigations it deems necessary regarding any environmental issues relating to the purchase including and without limitation whether the property complies with all environmental laws of any local authority, state government or federal government or any other statutory or government authority within 21 days from the date of this Contract and the Buyer being satisfied with the results, failing which the Buyer will be entitled to terminate this Contract. In that event this matter will be at an end, the deposit refunded to the Buyer and neither party will have a claim against the other apart from any rights either of the parties will have against the other as a result of any breach of this Contract prior to termination.
>
> The Seller will allow the Buyer and its consultants, agents and representatives access to the property before settlement during business hours Monday to Friday upon giving reasonable notice that they require access to allow them to carry out any enquiries and investigations.

This clause has been inserted for the benefit of the Buyer and may be waived by notice in writing to the Seller at any time before settlement."

52 WHEN IS FIRE SAFETY AN ISSUE?

A first-time investor wanted my advice about things to look out for when buying older wooden buildings and homes. I advised him that if you're purchasing a wooden building, for example a backpackers complex or a house that was once an old miner's cottage, it's vital that the contract be subject to you carrying out a check about fire safety matters.

A suitable clause would be:

> "This Contract is subject to the Buyer undertaking any enquiries and investigations it deems necessary regarding any fire safety issues relating to the purchase including and without limitation whether the property complies with all fire safety laws of any local authority, state government or federal government or any other statutory or government authority within 21 days from the date of this Contract and the Buyer being satisfied with the results, failing which the Buyer will be entitled to terminate this Contract.
>
> In that event this matter will be at an end, the deposit refunded to the Buyer and neither party will have a claim against the other apart from any rights either of the parties will have against the other as a result of any breach of this Contract prior to termination. The Seller agrees to allow the Buyer and its consultants, contractors, agents and

representatives access to the property before settlement during business hours Monday to Friday upon giving them reasonable notice that they require access to allow them to carry out any enquiries.

This clause has been inserted for the benefit of the Buyer and may be waived by notice in writing to the Seller at any time before settlement."

53 HOW IMPORTANT IS IT TO DO A SURVEY ON A PROPERTY?

A middle-aged client flung off the shackles of the "victim mentality" and enrolled in an Anthony Robbins course. Inspired by the big man himself, he decided to take "massive action" (Anthony Robbins' words) and purchased a block of vacant land on which to construct a duplex. His goal was to build two quality units, sell off the better one of the two and use the net proceeds of the sale to reduce the mortgage on the other unit to a level where the property was positively geared. He would retain that unit as an investment.

Every council in Australia has a minimum lot size requirement for unit developments and in this case it was 400 m^2 of land per lot. The contract of sale showed the property having an area of 810 m^2, 10 m^2 to spare for a two-unit development – or so my client thought.

After settlement it was revealed the property was only 790 m^2 and he wasn't entitled to build two units, but instead could only build a single-dwelling house.

Oh no!

What he'd planned to be a long-term buy and hold of a positively-geared property had now turned into a negative-gearing situation.

The moral of the story?

In these circumstances, always make the contract subject to a survey to verify the area of the property being purchased.

54 HOW DO I CHECK WHO REALLY OWNS THE PLANT AND EQUIPMENT ON THIS FARM I AM BUYING?

A client of mine signed up to buy a small farm and as settlement date drew closer he visited the property to meet the seller to discuss buying some of the plant and equipment on the farm, namely the tractor, motorbike and ride-on mower. He told me he left that meeting with an agreement in principle to purchase all of this equipment, subject to him checking out that it was reasonable value with second-hand dealers.

He was then contacted by the selling agent who advised him that the ex-partner of the female vendor (the property was being sold following their separation) had called to ask the agent whether the equipment was included in the sale. At that stage the agent didn't know of the agreement in principle and advised the caller that it wasn't. The seller's ex-partner then said, "Good, it belongs to me, I'll be coming to collect it after settlement."

The agent's next call was to my client who then phoned me to ask whether it was still safe to purchase this equipment from the female seller. I advised him it wasn't because he was now aware of a claim over this property. He suggested getting a letter from the seller confirming that she had ownership of this equipment. Would this solve the problem? My advice was that it wouldn't. He had now been put on notice of a claim by someone else for this equipment and the only safe thing to do, regardless of assurances by the female seller, was to buy new equipment.

55 SHOULD I BE CONCERNED ABOUT FLOODS AND OTHER NATURAL DISASTERS?

Flooding ravaged the property world in many parts of Australia in 2011. Floods decimated values, blew out insurance costs and what landlords up till then had thought were longstanding leases, were terminated by tenants. This is to say nothing of the impact on the amount of rent paid.

If we have learnt anything as investors from these natural disasters it is this.

If you buy a property in a town that has ever been affected by flooding you are a fool to yourself and a burden to others unless you make the contract subject to a flooding check. Here is the clause that you need. Add it to your investor's toolbox.

> "This Contract is subject to the Buyer satisfying himself within (complete) days from the date of the Contract that the property has not in the past been affected by flooding.
>
> If the Buyer determines that the property has in the past been flooded then the Buyer may terminate this Contract by notice in writing to the Seller but in order to be able to do so that notice must be accompanied by a written statement from the local authority or a registered surveyor stating that, or to the effect that, the land has in the past been affected by flooding. In that event the deposit will be refunded to the Buyer and after that neither party will have any claim against the other apart from a claim based on rights either of the parties may have against the other as a result of any breach of this Contract prior to termination."

In other parts of Australia at other times, bush-fires and drought have caused similar problems. Due diligence should be conducted in these circumstances too and a clause drafted to protect you until it has been completed.

"Why should I learn algebra? I've no intention of ever going there."
BILLY CONNOLLY, SCOTTISH COMEDIAN

Part IX
SMART QUESTIONS ABOUT LEASES AND TENANCIES

Rivers: Come on, Joan, tell us which husband was the best lover.
Collins: Yours.

JOAN RIVERS AND JOAN COLLINS

Smart Questions About Leases and Tenancies

Passing of possession of a property by giving over the keys, symbolises the change of its ownership. This is reflected in a standard provision, used in almost every master contract used for property sales, which states that on settlement the seller will deliver vacant possession of the property to the buyer unless the existence of a lease is disclosed in the contract of sale.

Despite the fundamental importance then of passing possession of the property and the terms of any lease, this is an issue that is often overlooked or not dealt with properly in a contract of sale.

This is particularly the case where the selling agent is different from the letting agent. And why is this? The answer is that the letting agent may have been dutifully managing the letting of the property over the last seven years, say, in the hope that one day they will secure appointment to sell the property along with neighbouring properties – and perhaps even handle the eventual sale of a small block of units on the site.

Unfortunately, however, for the letting agent, the new girl in town, fresh from her real estate agency course and through beginner's luck, ends up selling the property unexpectedly. So the psychology at play here is that the letting agent will often be very offended that they were not even given the chance to list the sale of the property and there will therefore be little co-operation, to say the least, between the letting agent and the selling agent, particularly about disclosure of the full terms of the lease. Quite often the existence of an option to extend the lease will not be disclosed to a buyer and this can become a major impediment to the settlement, or the subject of serious litigation between the buyer and seller following settlement.

It is therefore in your interest as an investor to be more aware of this issue and much can be learnt from the questions in this part of the book. So read on and replace your ignorance with knowledge and you will become even stronger as an investor. Working in ignorance (and without education) disarms your ability to be successful and often can derail the transaction. Once you are educated, though, you are back on the real estate highway and mobilised to take action to avoid something that would have otherwise been a road block.

> *"Any man who has $10,000 left when he dies is a failure."*
> ERROL FLYNN, ACTOR

56 I AM BUYING A PROPERTY WITH A TENANT – WHAT ARE THE TRAPS?

A well-informed and educated investor will always call for a copy of the lease to check the representations made by the seller and the seller's agent and, in particular, to check whether the lease contains any options. Options are nearly always for the benefit of the tenant. That is, it is the tenant's call about whether they exercise the option to extend the lease and no input or approval from the landlord is required.

If a copy of the lease is not available at the time you sign the contract, make sure you include a clause that makes it compulsory for the seller to provide you with a copy of the lease and ensure that the contract is subject to you approving the terms of this lease. Alternatively, make the contract subject to checking that the lease matches the representations made by the seller and the seller's agent. A sample clause would be:

> "The Seller agrees to produce to the Buyer or the Buyer's solicitors within two working days from the date of this Contract a copy of the current lease and all alterations, variations and extensions to it. This Contract is subject to the Buyer being satisfied with the terms of this lease within five working days of the Buyer or its solicitor receiving a copy of the lease, failing which the Buyer will be entitled to end this matter, the deposit will be refunded to the Buyer and neither party will have any claim against the other apart from a claim based upon a breach of the Contract by the other party prior to the date of termination."

57 SHOULD I ALLOW THE SELLER TO REMAIN IN POSSESSION AFTER SETTLEMENT?

All too often, sellers of property wish to stay on for the short to medium term following settlement and they are more than happy to pay a realistic rent for the property. The new owner of the property may be happy to accommodate them but may not wish to lock themselves into a formal lease for such a short-term arrangement where consumer protection laws in most states heavily favour the tenant.

The way to go is for the seller to stay on under a licence. That is a revocable contractual right between the buyer and the seller which isn't subject to the consumer protection tenancy legislation and can simply be cancelled on a short period of notice (seven days). If you find yourself in a situation as a buyer or seller, and are looking for a clause to add to the contract to deal with this issue, a sample clause that you could use is as follows:

> "The Vendor shall have the right to remain in possession of the property following Settlement for a maximum period of three months provided they make payment of all electricity and telephone charges and continue to insure the property to the Vendor's satisfaction. The Vendor agrees before Settlement to execute a licence regarding their occupation of the property following Settlement, such licence to be prepared by the Purchaser's solicitors at the Purchaser's expense and without limitation, such licence shall include the following provisions:
>
> The Vendor must maintain the property in substantially its

condition at the date of Settlement, fair wear and tear excepted;

Entry into possession is personal to the Vendor and is revocable at any time by the Purchaser giving the Vendor seven days' notice in writing and does not create a relationship of landlord and tenant.

The Vendor indemnifies the Purchaser against any expense, damages, claims, action or proceedings taken by the Vendor or any other party against the Purchaser as a result of the Vendor's possession of the property."

58 IS IT TRUE THAT THE LEASE OF A COMMERCIAL PROPERTY IS EVERYTHING?

As many readers would understand, commercial properties are sold on their yield. That is, if the property has a tenant paying $100,000 net rent and the market is experiencing sales at a yield of 10 per cent, then the sale price for this property would be around $1 million. The tenant, and therefore the lease, is everything with commercial properties.

It's vital, then, to have your solicitor check the validity of the lease when you buy a commercial property so that you're fully aware of the terms of the lease, including the balance of the term.

I recently fielded a call from the seller of a small commercial property which comprised three tenancies. The contract of sale disclosed the existence of these three tenancies, one of which was at a rental of $2,600 per calendar month with the lease expiring two years from settlement. The contract was dated October 31, 2007 and settled on November 30, 2007.

After settlement the buyer's solicitor wrote to my firm on behalf of the new owner advising that the tenant had in fact ceased trading in November 2007 and returned the keys to my client's agent at the end of that month. The buyer, through his solicitor, alleged that we had misrepresented the lease to him or alternatively misled and deceived him about the real position with the tenant. He claimed $2,600 per month in the interim for lost rent until an alternative tenant was found, and if one wasn't found, or was found for a lesser rent, then the buyer claimed the capital loss to him because of the reduced rental position (remember commercial properties are sold and valued on yield). The seller claimed he had no knowledge whatsoever about the tenant vacating the premises as it occurred on settlement date. He maintained that the agent hadn't informed him and therefore he had no responsibility.

My advice to him was that as his agent had knowledge of the matter, he was deemed to know and I believed that he had a duty to disclose this development to the buyer. If he had disclosed this new development, could the buyer have terminated the contract? In this circumstance I think not, as the contract (as is the case with most commercial contracts) didn't contain a warranty that the lease would be current and the tenant not in default on settlement. In the circumstances of this sale, the contract contained a due diligence clause which made the contract subject to the buyer and their solicitor undertaking a due diligence on the property and, in particular, on the status and validity of the leases.

If the seller or the agent had knowledge of the default by the tenant during the due diligence period, and hadn't disclosed this to the buyer by no later than the expiration of the due diligence period, then I advised my client that the buyer would have a genuine claim for misleading and deceptive conduct. Otherwise, as had occurred here, if the default had occurred after the expiration of the due diligence and before settlement, in the absence of a clause warranting that on settlement all leases would be valid and current, the risk of this development occurring rested squarely with the buyer.

The moral of the story is this: if you're buying a commercial property, make enquiries with the letting agent about the status of the leases and check the tenants aren't in default before your contract is signed, or at least during the due diligence period. Better still, visit the tenant yourself and ask them about their long-term plans.

59 IS IT HARD TO SACK YOUR LETTING AGENT

Let's say that after much research you've selected a person you believe to be competent, professional and experienced to manage your rental properties.

You got the appointment wrong last time by engaging someone who was good at presenting themselves, but had over-promised and under-delivered.

It all sounds good now, though, as you have a new agent. Or is it?

You must remember that the single most important thing about engaging someone to manage your property is the ability to move them on and engage another if your experience with them doesn't work out.

All too often, the standard documentation produced by the real estate industry for their members (i.e. the letting agents, and not you the investor) provides that 60 to 90 days' notice must be given to terminate an appointment as an agent.

But you are free to shorten that period!

On many occasions I have reduced that period down to 14 days' notice to terminate or, at worst, 30 days. I've never had a real estate agent push back on this point and at the end of the day they'll accept a much reduced period if you are educated enough to know to state that in the agreement.

If you hadn't really thought about this issue before, but now find yourself wondering how you can move on your letting agent rather than having to wait out a 90 day notice period, the answer is with a cheque.

The problem with waiting out this period is that the incompetent agent can do a lot more damage by the time their 90 day notice period runs out. At the end of the day you can terminate the arrangement earlier than, say, 90 days, but it will trigger a claim by the agent for compensation for the lost commission for the 90-day period. The claim will only usually run into hundreds of dollars and is small beer compared to the damage and loss that can occur if you leave the property with a negligent and incompetent letting agent. So pay it and move on.

> *"Journalist: What effect on history do you think it would have made if, in 1963, President Khruschev had been assassinated instead of President Kennedy?*
>
> *Mikhail Gorbachev: With history one can never be certain, but I think I can confidently say that Aristotle Onassis would not have married Mrs Khrushchev."*
>
> MIKHAIL GORBACHEV

Part X
MORE SMART QUESTIONS

There was no respect for youth when I was young, and now that I am old there is no respect for age. I missed it coming and going.

ANONYMOUS, BUT TROUBLED

More Smart Questions

You come now to the last part of this book which deals with a range of topics that don't easily fit elsewhere. Nonetheless, the answers to this grab-bag of questions illuminate the world of the property investor and where there was darkness, the answers reveal light. So add them all to your tool-box as a property investor as education builds a confidence that will embolden and even enrich you.

> *"The difference between tax avoidance and tax evasion is the thickness of the prison wall."*
> DENIS HEALY, BRITISH LABOUR POLITICIAN

60 HOW CAN I GET ACCESS TO A PROPERTY BEFORE THE SETTLEMENT DATE?

If you are purchasing a property to renovate or redevelop then "time is money". It is important that from the date you settle you are in a position to proceed immediately with the renovations or redevelopment as "run-ons" can be expensive. You should therefore include a clause in your offer to purchase that gives you access immediately upon signing the contract. A suggested clause would be as follows:

> "In order to allow the Buyer to take measurements and obtain quotes for renovation and building work which they propose to carry out following completion, the Seller agrees to allow the Buyer access to the property before settlement during business hours Monday to Friday upon giving a minimum of 24 hours' notice to the Seller or the Seller's agent."

61 WHAT ARE MY RIGHTS AS A BUYER OF A PROPERTY TO GET AN EARLY SETTLEMENT?

It is important as a buyer to have the right to complete early for many commercial reasons. You don't want your ability to do so to be frustrated by a seller who may be too lazy to meet your timetable. It is a common misconception among buyers and sellers of real estate and businesses that where the contract provides for settlement "on or before" a date, this gives either party the right to complete the sale earlier than that date. It does not.

In order to have the right to settle early, a special condition must be added. A suitable clause would be:

> "The Buyer will have the right to settle early, on a date to be nominated by it provided that it gives to the Seller 30 days' notice in writing that it requires such an early settlement and it nominates in that notice the earlier date for settlement."

62 WHAT RISK DO I CARRY AS A BUYER OF A PROPERTY AFTER THE CONTRACT IS SIGNED?

In almost every state in Australia the risk of any damage to the property passes very quickly from the seller to the buyer – within a day or two of formation of the contract of sale. Buyers should therefore take out a "cover" note (i.e. interim insurance to protect their position should some damage occur to the property before settlement), as they will have to take the property with the burden of that damage. In some cases, it may not be possible to get a cover note for the property. In such cases, it would be advisable to insert a clause similar to the following so that the risk of any damage to the property remains with the seller until settlement.

> "Regardless of any other clause in this Contract, the property is at the Seller's risk from the date of this contract until settlement date."

63. I HAVE BEEN ASKED TO BE A TOKEN DIRECTOR OF MY FRIEND'S COMPANY – WHAT DO YOU THINK?

This query was timely, given the changing economics over the first three months of 2008. My client had been asked by an old and dear friend to become a "token" director in her investment company. For certain reasons that aren't relevant here, my client's friend couldn't be a director of her own company, although she was the sole shareholder. She told my client that the job was just a "rubber stamp" and all of the management and work of the company would be done by her.

My client was keen to help out here, as her old friend had assisted her financially and personally many times over their long friendship. My client ultimately accepted on the basis that the company and her friend personally indemnified her against any claims that could be made in future against her as a director.

For those interested readers I have set out below an extract from the Deed of Indemnity for your education.

> "(Insert name of sole shareholder) indemnifies (insert name of director) against all claims, actions and proceedings for any loss and damage incurred or arising out of the director acting as a director including the performance or non-performance of all duties imposed upon her at law as director of the company or her failure, neglect or omission to perform any such duties other than through fraud or dishonesty of the director."

In the circumstances it probably wasn't a great commercial risk to take, particularly if you base it on the prosperity that the investment and property world has enjoyed over recent years. Good economic times often forgive a lot of financial mistakes. But the times were a-changing.

The subprime crisis loomed large over the financial world in 2008 (about $100 billion in loans were due for refinancing in March of that year), the United States economy bordered on a recession (it then had an annual growth rate of less than 1 per cent) and our new political masters were conditioning us daily at the time about the inevitability of interest rate increases.

Historically, tougher times see an increase in the number of liquidations and this leads to an increase in recovery action by liquidators and creditors against directors of companies, *including* nominee or shadow directors. These directors are a target when liquidators and creditors claim payment from directors because of insolvent trading by the company (where the directors allow the company to continue to trade where there weren't reasonable grounds to believe that the company could pay its debts as they fell due). It isn't a defence to a claim that you're only a de-facto director and that you left the running and operation of the company to your old friend. If that were the case, the liquidator could make a claim based on a breach of director's duties in not acting in good faith (by just "rubber stamping" decisions by the sole shareholder who controlled the company). So, while acting as a director of someone else's company was always something you would only do in exceptional circumstances, in our changing times much more discernment and wisdom is needed in considering a request to do so.

64 TIRED OF THE TREADMILL OF BUY, RENOVATE, SELL – IS IT REALLY ALL WORTH IT?

An exhausted beginner investor called me to say that after only three buy, renovate and sell deals they had had enough. They now wanted their life back and had signed to buy a new house in a prime position in a new subdivision developed by a major house/land developer. Everything was brand new (and finished). They had done their homework and were confident that the strong capital growth enjoyed by this area over recent years would continue unabated. No more of the blood sweat and toil of spending all of their quality personal time "on the tools". "This property", they said, "would make them money while they were sleeping."

The first year of ownership was going well, so far, with the investors having every expectation that double-digit capital growth was going to be the order of the day. Then, kaboom!! The sky fell in.

The developer, obviously unsatisfied with sales of its new stock, released without warning onto the market a flood of new homes (with more to come) at prices that matched those paid one to two years earlier. This area now had a continuous supply of houses for up to the next two years. Beastly careless to the bleating from my clients and other buyers of the house and land packages who had bought with the same strategy as my client, the developer pushed on with his release of the properties to the marketplace. My client's dreams of living in capital gains heaven were now swapped with the harsh reality of a life of meeting mortgage payments month after month for years to come for no reward.

The moral of the story is this. When buying from a developer be aware that until it has sold the last of its stock it controls the price (and therefore capital growth) of properties in that area. It can limit that supply by feeding new stock onto the market and keep the demand for new stock and prices high. Alternatively, as in this case, it can flood the market to ensure that its cash flow is high thus depressing values for some time to come.

65 THIS DEVELOPMENT SITE HAS GONE UP SO MUCH. SHOULD I JUST SELL IT AND FORGET DEVELOPING IT?

A developer was faced with a dilemma. Five months earlier, he'd purchased two large lots of land on which he planned to construct a unit development. The contracts were now unconditional with settlement in 90 days' time. He had a hard decision to make.

The properties had gone up so much in value that he now tossed up whether to proceed with his development or whether to cash in his equity and just on-sell the properties. He opted for the latter. His first question was, could he place the properties on the market now and settle his purchase simultaneously with his sale? Or did he have to first settle the purchase, thereby throwing away some substantial stamp duty costs?

I told him yes, he could list the property for sale now, but he couldn't represent to potential buyers that he was the owner of the properties. He had to instruct the selling agent to tell buyers that he has the property secured by unconditional contracts but that he wanted to on-sell them with hopefully simultaneous settlements. That is, the on-purchaser would settle on the same day that he was required to settle, using the ultimate purchaser's funds to pay out the purchase price payable on the blocks.

My client would ride off into the sunset with a bank cheque in his back pocket and "goodbye" would be all he said. I also advised him to ensure that when he engaged the agent to sell the property, he amended the 'Standard Authority to Sell' to change the usual guarantee that he owns the properties to a warranty that he had the properties under unconditional contracts.

The final question my client had was, "Can I put a For Sale sign on the properties now?" The simple answer was no. Under the standard contract, possession of the property (and therefore the right to erect a sign) remains with the seller until settlement, when possession then passes to the buyer. There was nothing to stop him, however, from approaching the owner through the agent to get permission to erect a sign advertising the properties as being for sale. Most reasonable sellers would agree to such a request.

66 DEPRECIATION AND NEGATIVE GEARING – ARE THE BENEFITS REALLY JUST A MYTH?

An annoyed investor who owned a number of investment properties rang me recently with a gripe. She prided herself on having a good general knowledge of tax and legal matters and was startled to learn from a fellow investor that all the depreciation she'd been claiming over the properties over the past five years, and the negative gearing losses on two of the properties, would have to be repaid to the Tax Office if she ever sold the properties. As her friend put it, "What Caesar giveth, Caesar also taketh away."

Her question to me, of course, was whether this claim was correct. I advised that so far as the negative gearing losses were concerned, her fellow investor's claim was not correct. He did, however, have a point in relation to the depreciation. The building depreciation on the construction costs, (and not the depreciation on things such as fittings or whitegoods) was effectively repaid on the sale of the property. The way it works is that in calculating the taxable profit on the sale of the property (i.e. capital gain), the purchase price and holding costs (i.e. cost base) is reduced by the amount of the building depreciation claims over the time she owned the property. Much relieved she said, "Phew, I can live with that. It's not as big a hit as I thought".

67 HOW DOES GST AFFECT A VALUATION?

An excited client rang me to advise that I'd be receiving material for him shortly to purchase a unit at almost 10 per cent below a sworn valuation. When the documentation arrived, the valuation showed the unit to have a value of $440,000, comprising $400,000 for a newly renovated unit plus $40,000 for GST. My client had been misled. A basic understanding of tax and GST law would reveal that this unit, because it was newly renovated, is regarded as "new residential premises" and unlike established residential premises, it attracted GST on the sale price. When I raised this issue with the developer he advised that the true value of the unit was as per the valuation, that is $440,000, and my client was therefore buying it at a discounted price to the tune of $40,000. He said: "When the sale is recorded at the Titles Office, it will show a sale price of $440,000, the same as the valuation."

The point my client had missed, which I made to the developer, was that if my client had to realise this asset and sell it, even immediately after settlement of the sale to him, it would then be regarded as established residential premises and would be GST-free. If the valuation provided by the developer was correct this would result in a sale for $400,000. The fundamental error my client was making was that he was accepting a valuation undertaken on the basis it was GST-inclusive, whereas an astute investor would have discounted this valuation and only accepted the valuation on the basis it was GST-exclusive. The latter is the way an astute investor would look at it because this is how they'd sell the property when they go to the market.

I recall that when GST law was first introduced this was a major issue within the valuation profession and the practice has now evolved amongst valuers, so that when valuing units in new buildings they carefully research recent on-sales in similar buildings by the first purchaser. That is, they look at resales in that building and sales in other comparable established buildings (after the developer has sold) to determine the value.

68 THIS DEVELOPER HAS DA APPROVAL, BUT NOW WANTS TO SELL WITHOUT DEVELOPING. HOW CAN I PICK UP THE BENEFIT OF THIS DA APPROVAL IF I NOW BUY OFF THE DEVELOPER?

Investors at all levels in any marketplace have second thoughts and even get "cold feet" proceeding with investment purchases, and in particular real estate developments.

One group of client companies found itself in the situation where it had obtained approval to construct a large commercial development on a substantial block of land. The issue of the development permit from council was imminent and it had spent about $100,000 in undertaking due diligence enquiries, a feasibility, preparation of a development application (DA) and subdivision application to the local council. This was without factoring anything in for its time and effort in getting the development to that stage. The economic slowdown then started to bite.

So that it could survive to see another day as a developer it decided to rationalise its developments and jettison this particular one. The lucky buyer purchased this property without the expense, risk, uncertainty or delay that the companies that owned it had experienced, and bought it with the benefit of the DA. It therefore was vital from the buyer's point of view that it took a transfer of the benefit of all of the works plans and approvals, etc. and this requirement was the genesis of the following clause:

"a. The Seller warrants that they have carried out or commissioned works, tests, plans, drawings, designs, analysis, bills, applications, advertising, reports and other matters (called the "works") details of which are set out in Annexure "B" at its expense and it is the owner of or holds the benefit of such works, as the case may be;

b. The Seller warrants that it has paid for the costs of completing and carrying out the works and agrees to deliver to the Buyer within seven days of the date of this contract, confirmation in writing from each of the persons or companies that undertook the works that payment has been made to them in full of all the costs and expenses incurred;

c. The benefit of and ownership of the works are passed to the Buyer on settlement and the Seller will deliver to the Buyer on settlement all documentation for the works including and without limitation the originals of all tests, plans, drawings, designs, analysis, applications and reports and all of its obligations under this clause are a fundamental term of the contract which have been inserted for the benefit of the Buyer, any part or all of which may be waived by the Buyer in writing on or before settlement.

d. The Seller will retain the original tax invoices for the carrying out of the works and in particular the Seller will retain the right to claim any tax credits for any GST payable in relation to the invoices."

69 PERSONAL GUARANTEES – WHAT DO I NEED TO CHECK?

If the buyer of your property is a company, then be aware that a company is a separate legal entity from its directors and shareholders and you should consider whether to insist that the directors of the buyer company personally guarantee the company's performance of its obligations under the contract. This is especially important if there's only a token or nominal deposit paid, as was the case with a new client of our firm.

As an inexperienced investor (he was selling the only investment property he had ever owned), he was wise to consult a property solicitor about the terms of the contract before he signed it. The purchase price was around $400,000 and in this part of the world such purchase contracts usually show a deposit of 5 per cent of the purchase price ($20,000) or ideally 10 per cent ($40,000). In this case the deposit was only 2 per cent ($8,000) – coincidently, the exact amount of the agent's commission. The agent had promoted the contract to him as one that was unconditional – settlement in 30 days' time and the buyer was a company well known to the agent as it had purchased other properties from the agency.

We advised our client that the purpose of the deposit was to act as "hurt money" and provided the security that the buyer would perform its obligations under the contract. With a deposit of only $8,000, if the buyer defaulted and didn't settle this matter, the deposit would be forfeited (under the terms of most engagements of agents this money will be paid to the agent and not the seller) and the seller's only option would be to consider whether to pursue a company which might have no other assets. Most sellers would simply walk away. If, however, the directors of that company were personally responsible for the buyer company's default (because they'd signed personal guarantees) then the company may think long and hard about whether to walk away from the deal and expose the directors to personal liability. Our advice to our client, therefore, was that the buyer should either increase the deposit to at least 5 per cent of the purchase price or ideally 10 per cent, and/or provide personal guarantees before he sold the property to that company.

70 TRADING PROPERTIES – WHAT ARE THE PITFALLS FOR THE UNWARY?

I received a call from an investor who had been sitting on an old fibro cottage in an area which he thought would be a prime redevelopment site. He had been watching prices rise and rise but in the past year or two they'd slipped back. He didn't find this out until he put the property on the market at what he thought would be a record price, only to find out that the market hadn't rang a bell when it hit the top, and he'd missed the upswing.

Keen to sell the property, but with unrealistic expectations about its value, he placed an ad in the exchanges and trades section in the real estate part of his local newspaper. As luck would have it he found someone with a similar problem and he agreed to exchange his property for another person's expensive unit. The exchange got him out of a property that he no longer wanted but he didn't have the cash from the sale to, for example, pay his capital gains tax. I also gave him a fright when I told him the amount of stamp duty he'd have to pay on the expensive unit that he was trading.

He then suggested to me that we should "write down" purchase prices of both properties to save him and his co-investor a bit of stamp duty and a lot of tax. Wrong. My advice to him was this was a definite no-no and I strongly urged him not to do it. The reasons I gave him were as follows:

1. Firstly, writing down the purchase prices deprives the Australian Tax Office of revenue and this is considered fraud.

2. Secondly, the Office of State Revenue is entitled to stamp duty on the purchase price of the traded property or its value, whichever is the greater, and by writing down the purchase prices he will deprive them of revenue.

3. Thirdly, as he was transferring a loan from the fibro dwelling to the unit this created all sorts of problems for him and his lender. Lenders base the amount they're advancing on the value of the property or the purchase price – whichever is the lesser. If he wrote down the value, the lender wouldn't be able to transfer the full amount of the loan that he had on the fibro cottage over to the new unit.

4. Finally, and possibly worst of all, you artificially create a lower cost base for capital gains tax purposes which could come back to haunt you in the future. For example, if you wrote down the value of a property which was valued at $600,000 to a $400,000 sale price and you later sold the property after it had gained $200,000 (making it now worth $800,000), tax would be payable on the amount of $400,000 ($800,000 less $400,000). This is a huge mistake and the investor wanted to do it to save himself a miserable amount of stamp duty. Forget it!

71 WHAT ITEMS ARE INCLUDED IN THE SALE?

An investor purchased a property bordering on a national park. The house was a wooden structure and the lounge-room in particular was heavily decorated in wood panelling to blend in with the forest theme of the area. When the investor inspected the property prior to signing a contract he noticed that even the sound system continued the wood theme, with the sound speakers enclosed in quality teak wood casings, each two metres tall.

On settlement, the investor was horrified to find that the wood panelled speakers hadn't been left by the seller. He made a hurried phone call to the seller to explain they had mistakenly taken the speakers which were included in the sale. The seller told the investor "he needed a few more runs around the block" and should read what he signed.

When the investor did so he agreed with the seller. Despite his expectations to the contrary, the sale didn't include the sound speakers as they weren't noted as an inclusion in the contract. A simple check of the contract by a street-smart investor or their solicitor would have revealed this omission and the matter could have been dealt with at the time of signing the contract. The investor berated himself for his naivety and mentally reminded himself to be more careful in the future. The investor had the last say, however, when he wrote to the vendor to apologise for the upset about the speakers. He then went on in the same letter to tell the seller that he wanted to say thank you for their generosity for leaving the water in the swimming pool. Boom boom! The seller either took that one right between the eyes or it went right over their head.

72 SHOULD I CONSIDER A TEMPTING NEW FINANCIAL PRODUCT?

A client called me excitedly about a new financial product (loan) she thought would double the number of properties she could buy. The interest rate on the new product was 6 per cent per annum; the lender would agree to accept 3 per cent now with the balance of the 3 per cent capitalised onto the amount of the loan (that is, the interest added on to the amount borrowed).

The finance broker promoting the idea told her the lender would lend the monies to finance the purchase of properties on this basis in areas where there has historically been stable and steady capital growth in the property market because the likely future capital growth would be more than the amount of interest that was being capitalised. In addition, my client was told that the whole of the interest (that is, the 3 per cent payable now and the 3 per cent payable in the future) would be tax-deductible. She was keen to get going and use this facility promoted by the broker, as this would give her a massive leg up in becoming a property millionaire.

What the broker had clearly not mentioned was the risk involved in this strategy. I can understand why an investor would use such a product for part of their property portfolio, but to do it for all of your property investments, or even for a large percentage of it, is a risky affair. The whole strategy is based on "mortgaging the future". That is, if there was capital growth then the strategy would work just fine, but if it didn't materialise and the lender revalued the properties as they do regularly every few years, the investor would find themselves at the end of the "margin call". This is a requirement from the lender that they inject more money to increase their equity in the property because the property hadn't grown in value as it had done historically.

Those of you who invest in the sharemarket using geared products will know all too well the risks involved in margin calls. A drop in the value of a geared share portfolio because of a correction in the stock market has seen many an investor have to reluctantly inject capital or, worse still, sell down some of their portfolio.

Another downside to the strategy is that it locks you into the one broker and one lender.

73 POWERS OF ATTORNEY – DO I NEED ONE?

If you're involved in a property sale as a purchaser or seller and you're relying on other people to sign documents on your behalf then make sure you have a Power of Attorney registered in the state in which the property is located. As a solicitor on the Gold Coast I deal with people from all over Australia who often hold Powers of Attorney from others in that state, but that Power of Attorney can't be used to sign important documents, such as mortgages and transfers, unless it's actually registered in the state in which the property is situated. So, if you've entered into a real estate transaction and are heading off overseas, don't leave the execution of these important documents to others without giving your solicitor a call first to check everything is in order with your Power of Attorney.

74 BREAKDOWN OF APPLIANCES BEFORE SETTLEMENT – WHO IS RESPONSIBLE?

What's your position when you buy a property and everything in it, including security alarms, air conditioning units, intercom systems, etc., is in perfect order at the time you signed the contract, but before settlement an electrical storm causes them to stop working? Does the seller have to repair them so that they're left to you on settlement in good working order?

Most residential contracts provide that the risk of anything happening to the property (and everything included with the property) passes to the buyer on the date of the contract or a very short time afterwards. The risk of such damage usually therefore passes to a buyer and unless you're insured for it (that is, you've taken out interim insurance at the time you signed the contract in the form of a cover note), then it's your funeral and not the seller's.

It's possible, however – but not usual – to include a clause in the contract whereby the seller guarantees that all of the appliances and equipment will be in good working order at settlement.

75 WHAT STATE SHOULD THE PROPERTY BE IN ON SETTLEMENT?

Most contracts used throughout Australia simply provide that the property is to be passed to the buyer on settlement in the same condition it was in at the date that they inspected it. Unless you've taken clear photos of the interior of the property or videoed the interior, a dispute about the condition of the property and its cleanliness is likely to amount to nothing and you'll simply be left to clean up any mess the seller has left. If it's important to you that the property is left in a neat and tidy state you can include a clause in the contract to this effect. The clause must go further than simply providing that the seller must leave the property in a neat and tidy condition, as the seller may be a young male whose idea of clean and tidy is poles apart from the opinion of the middle-aged mother who's buying the property.

The property should be cleaned by professional cleaners to put the matter beyond any doubt and a sample clause that could be used is as follows:

> "The seller must, at its expense before settlement, ensure that all rubbish and debris is removed from the property and that the improvements on the property and the land will be transferred to the buyer on settlement in a neat, clean and tidy condition. In particular and without limitation the seller will at its expense before completion have all the interior of the residential dwelling on the property cleaned by professional cleaners, all carpets cleaned by professional carpet cleaners, and all rubbish and debris removed from the land."

So endeth the reading of the 23rd Psalm (if my recollection is correct, that is the one entitled "The Lord is my Shepherd".

How appropriate. Now that you have come to the very end of this book I want to encourage you to continue your education after you have turned this last page. As a property investor you need to become your own counsel. Whilst you can surround yourself with a team of professionals and mentors, at the end of the day you are alone and travelling on your own road as an investor seeking your fortune in the world of property. Your self-discipline in self-educating will see you through many crisEs with solutions that your education will bring forward for you. This self-education will build greater confidence and will ultimately develop courage, courage that does not fail you under stress.

> *"As a child my family's menu consisted of two choices: take it or leave it."*
>
> BUDDY HACKETT, AMERICAN COMEDIAN

Printed by Libri Plureos GmbH in Hamburg, Germany